"I didn't just read this book—I ⟨...⟩ *Tunnel of Grief* is raw and fecun⟨...⟩ funny, and razor sharp—one ⟨...⟩ navigation of the daily patho⟨...⟩ ⟨...⟩ry of the human condition. At times, the sheer craft of Jessica Hendry Nelson's writing stopped my breath and made me immediately re-read a passage just so that I could experience it again."

—**Emily Saliers**, Indigo Girls

"Jessica Hendry Nelson's *Joy Rides through the Tunnel of Grief* is a stunning, hilarious, propulsive book—somehow breathless and thoughtful at once—that I'll remember for the rest of my days. It is ruthlessly insightful but always merciful, never precious but always profound—written with a close, awestruck attention to the lush particulars of this world, its unexpected provisions of grace. It is full of surprising love songs—to gatherings of women, acts of caregiving and strange community, fraught friendships; to students and strange lessons; to various fruitful forms (the list, the letter, the shard); to the condition of loving flawed and self-thwarting people (all of us); and—most of all—to the terrifying, saving entanglement of suffering and wonder."

—**Leslie Jamison**, author of *The Recovering: Intoxication and Its Aftermath* and *The Empathy Exams*

"This raw and lyrical memoir beckons forth the all of life—birth, joy, death, grief—to posit wonder as a necessary means of survival. At once tender and devastating, I've never read anything like it."

—**Courtney Maum**, author of *The Year of the Horses*

"Jessica Hendry Nelson's *Joy Rides through the Tunnel of Grief* is a memoir of 'contradictory truths'—where a father is dead and alive all at once, where the past is as present as the word now in a world 'so full of love and longing and wonder and grief and fear.' It is an elegy. It is a love song. It is a cry to women to renew their bonds with one another. It is a sister's lament, and it is a dirge for a marriage gone under. It is also a book-length braided meditation on the act of creation itself—from the creation of life to the creation of story."

—**Brian Turner**, author of *My Life as a Foreign Country*

"For Jessica Hendry Nelson, the seams and edges of experience and feeling, the places most alive and frightening in their vulnerability, beauty, and rage are also places ripe with wonder. This is 'a book of impossible questions,' she writes. Beautifully wrought questions, I'd add—ones burnished by the intense beam of her attention. Among the most poignant: How to love those who are simultaneously here and not here? En route to her own true north, Nelson offers the very thing all readers yearn for: a heart's companion."

—**Lia Purpura**, author of *All the Fierce Tethers* and *It Shouldn't Have Been Beautiful*

"While—true to its name—this book certainly holds at its center the true gravity of real and anticipatory grief, unenviable but inevitable, Jessica Hendry Nelson's *Joy Rides through the Tunnel of Grief* thrums most with the urgency of life and wanting: to consume, to be consumed, to create, to destroy, and most of all to be salve and protection; more than anything, Nelson's writing explores with fearlessness and ferocity the urgent and unwavering pull to create despite the wake of male indecision and carelessness. Less a flattened portrayal of grief than a dimensional, contemporary portrait of what it is to exist as a woman in this world, Nelson's is an invigorating and refreshing testament to the competing pulls of love, fear, and desire."

—**Amy Butcher**, author of *Mothertrucker*

"*Joy Rides through the Tunnel of Grief* is the book I've been looking for on my shelf for decades. Nothing exists quite like it; it was the missing book. Compassionate, intellectual, surprising, and impeccably crafted, this memoir holds your darkest nights and most elated joys."

—**Chloe Caldwell**, author of *Women* and *The Red Zone*

JOY RIDES
THROUGH THE
TUNNEL OF GRIEF

THE **SUE WILLIAM SILVERMAN PRIZE**
FOR **CREATIVE NONFICTION**

JOY RIDES THROUGH THE TUNNEL OF GRIEF

A MEMOIR BY **JESSICA HENDRY NELSON**

THE UNIVERSITY OF GEORGIA PRESS ATHENS

The author acknowledges previous publication of the following works:
"Half Woman, Half Wonder," previously published as "Rapture of
the Deep" in *The Rumpus*; "In the End, We All Become Stories: Last
Letters to Jack," previously published as "When You Were a Boy in
Maine" in *Advanced Creative Nonfiction: A Writers' Guide and Anthology*
by Jessica Hendry Nelson and Sean Prentiss (Bloomsbury, 2021); and
"In the Valley," previously published in *North American Review*.

Published by the University of Georgia Press
Athens, Georgia 30602
www.ugapress.org
© 2023 by Jessica Hendry Nelson
All rights reserved
Designed by Kaelin Chappell Broaddus
Set in 10/13.5 Dolly Pro Regular by Kaelin Chappell Broaddus
Printed and bound by Sheridan Books, Inc.
The paper in this book meets the guidelines for permanence
and durability of the Committee on Production Guidelines
for Book Longevity of the Council on Library Resources.

Most University of Georgia Press titles are
available from popular e-book vendors.

Printed in the United States of America
23 24 25 26 27 P 5 4 3 2 1

Library of Congress Cataloging-in-Publication Data
Names: Nelson, Jessica Hendry, author.
Title: Joy rides through the tunnel of grief : a
memoir / by Jessica Hendry Nelson.
Description: Athens : The University of Georgia Press, 2023. |
Series: The Sue William Silverman prize for creative nonfiction
Identifiers: LCCN 2023007505 | ISBN 9780820365473 (paperback)
| ISBN 9780820365480 (epub) | ISBN 9780820365497 (pdf)
Subjects: LCSH: Nelson, Jessica Hendry. | Grief. |
Children of drug addicts—Biography.
Classification: LCC BF575.G7 N46 2023 | DDC 155.9/37—dc23/eng/20230415
LC record available at https://lccn.loc.gov/2023007505

For Eula James

There is no good answer to how to be a woman;
the art may instead lie in how we refuse the question.

—REBECCA SOLNIT

CONTENTS

ACKNOWLEDGMENTS

This book was made possible by the many women who continue to show up—for me, one another, and themselves—and model the real work of loving. Thank you to Susan Nelson, Helen Gordon, Jessie Mele, Hannah Campbell, Aryn Hood, Kara Fauth, and Rya Hardee-Fauth. Thank you also to Carole Gordon, Denise Gordon-Weisman, Adam Gordon, and Jean Berrier. Thank you to John Copenhaver, Greg Falla, Jon Mele, Mike and Mary Croley, Katherine Hurley, Sara Poindexter, Ellen Vitola, Lou Vitola, Debra Hoffman, Ashley McLaughlin, and the whole McLauglin family. Thank you to my friends and colleagues in the MFA program in creative writing at the University of Nebraska in Omaha, especially Teri Youmans Grimm, Tom Paine, and Karen Shoemaker. Thank you to the Ragdale Foundation, Buinho Creative Hub, and the Vermont Studio Center for the time, space, and inspiration. For the gift of their friendship and feedback on early drafts, my deepest gratitude to Sean Prentiss, Miciah Bay Gault, Andrew Merton, and Julia Shipley. For my current and former students at the University of Nebraska in Omaha MFA in creative writing; Vermont College of Fine Arts; Denison University; and Virginia Commonwealth University—you motivate and inspire me every day. This book exists in the world because of the brilliant feedback and unyielding support of my agent, Nicole Cunningham, at the Book Group. I am also grateful to the Association of Writers and Writing Programs, Sue William Silverman, and Brian Turner for the incredible gift of the Sue William

Silverman Prize in Creative Nonfiction. Thank you to the team at the University of Georgia Press for their tireless support. My big love always to my brother, Eric Nelson. And to Jessica Smith and Charlie Helen, thank you for expanding my heart.

To David, for everything I never thought possible, including our daughter.

JOY RIDES
THROUGH THE
TUNNEL OF GRIEF

[PROLOGUE]

I want to create a beautiful dying
The end will need to be dark and soft
Like walking home to your real mother
—MELISSA BRODER, from "Light Control"

MARCH 2020

The thing about the apocalypse is that nobody said it would be so beautiful.

Inside my mother's house outside of Philadelphia the muted TV ticks off unfathomable death tolls. People line up outside grocery stores bartering for toilet paper and Clorox wipes. The acrid tang of some invisible virus hangs in the air. Hospital corridors flush with hot, white panic, and refrigerated trucks, temporary body storage, fill parking lots. This mouth, a pith of rage, fills every other shot. It makes sounds, but not sense. On the coffee table are a pile of ripped pillowcases in various stages of transformation, glint of strewn sewing needles, black thread, an unused replacement filter for the air conditioner cut into twelve muzzle-sized strips.

Morning breaks on a kitchen, a woman, a mug that reads "Nice Tits" above illustrations of various birds: "Great Tit"; "Long-

Tailed Tit"; "Crested Tit." Her tits, she notices, are sweating through Kurt Cobain's pretty face on her thirty-year-old Nirvana T-shirt. Coffee pools on the countertop, trembling above the running dishwasher. She stares through the window. That stranger on the sidewalk in the yellow hat is a threat. That idling, white truck is a sign. The grocery store is a war zone. Any small intimacy a potential violence. Even the benign, one-eyed dog asleep on the floor is newly suspicious.

And yet.

Spring is letting down her hair.

The world splays open like a pocket mirror, the sky a pearl blue. Has anything ever been so bright? Smelled so sweet? This wet, briny soil. Neon green pomiformis moss holding court on garden rocks. Pink cherry blossoms canopying the front yard. New leaves are lime green, awash on the horizon. While I pour another cup of coffee, the one-eyed dog looks at me with disdain, then collapses on the floor. We hate mornings just the same.

Two weeks ago, Denison closed indefinitely, the small liberal arts university outside of Columbus, Ohio, where I teach creative writing. The day before shutdown, the students bounced through the halls like pinballs, floating in and out of my office, not sure the right questions to ask or what to do next. Of course, we had no answers. *Go home?* we shrugged. *Ask your mamas?* Surely, there were grownups prepared to handle this newest global humbling. No doubt they will soon emerge heroically from behind the curtain and tell us what to do. In the meantime, our news feeds tell us, we need only secure a few weeks' worth of canned goods and wine and to sit tight.

The cavalry is a 'coming, et cetera. Find ye a sourdough starter stat.

No one else is up yet, so I bring my coffee back to bed and pick up a book, my concerto as the ship goes down, a third space into which I shall serenely sink. I glimpse my mother's neighbor through the guest-room window, pregnant and sunning herself on the back porch. A red azalea glows behind her, almost blinding. Her languor belies her fortitude. She is not *graced* with child—as Saint Francis was blessed with the stigmata—but vigorously *at work*, like a glacier carving the surface of the earth. I've been watching her since I arrived at my mother's house a week ago. I watch her with hopes of learning something about how to be a woman. She weaves stars out of straw and hangs them from the eaves of her porch. Giant pink gladioli nod sleepily in the garden. She has a big job somewhere corporate-y, the details of which I know nothing. This is her first baby and, like me, she is past prime childbearing years. Maybe thirty-eight, forty. I am both heartened and blindly jealous of her fecundity. Her wife comes out and hands her a mug of something steaming, kisses the top of her head, and then returns inside. I turn over and pull the covers over my shoulders. Birds sing, the train wails in the distance, the dog barks at nothing. Life keeps setting off alarms. My phone, for example, is still ringing. No doubt it's the guy I've been dating for the last year who, I've recently discovered, has a raging temper and a wellspring of abandonment issues that make my shit look practically Buddhist. He's the reason I fled here from Columbus after it became clear we would not be returning to campus. He'd started to scare me, showing up at my apartment unannounced, shouting nonsensically and weeping on the front lawn. He'd been a nice reprieve after the divorce, though. A master of facades and the best sex of my life. He has two kids from a previous marriage who are old enough to make their own breakfasts, though they won't dare, and a manic adoration I'd happily mistaken for love.

Anyway, it's over now. In a few months, provided the job offer remains, I will move to Virginia to start a tenure-track teaching position. This is the big guns, the job I've been working toward forever, a chance to settle down, as they say. "They" being The Women, my mother and grandmother, Mommom, my two matriarchs, and by "settle down" they mean "Get remarried and have babies." The Women say, "You have plenty of time" but also "Tick tock." The one-eyed dog doesn't care one way or the other. He's as settled as an easy chair, snoring softly now, tail wagging gently in dream.

And, well, I'd tried to settle down. Fifteen years with the same person, a house in Vermont, a couple of years married. An idealized trajectory for a certain kind of young, white, middle-class woman in America. The kind of young, white, middle-class woman The Women would prefer me to be. The kind I had once preferred myself to be, had rather willfully set out to become. The trouble is that I failed spectacularly—and for many of the reasons that America herself fails: self-loathing, inherited grief, irrational fears, an indoctrinated attraction to emotionally absent men with a dysfunctional relationship to sex and power, et cetera, et cetera.

While I was ambivalent about kids, the husband was adamantly opposed. Perhaps "ambivalent" is too mild a word. I agonized, weighed, fantasized, and bartered. I pleaded with the husband to reconsider, but to no avail. Eventually, I realized I'd have to leave him if I wanted a child, so the making of new love would require the annihilation of another. I didn't like the idea of giving up love in order to create it. That math didn't add up. "Women are always looking for something to fill their holes," I read in a poem around that time. I filled my holes with rapacious love. Do you blame me? Women are told again and again that we are not enough. Holes, but not whole. We are born with our mother's grief inside us, and her mother's grief, and her mother's grief before her. To have children, then, is to pass on their grief like a torch that, if extinguished, ceases to *mean*. Why else would my mother remind me how difficult I was to raise? How hard she worked? About the coerced abortions she didn't want? How much she suffered and sacrificed? Of course, there were the many sundry sexual assaults she had endured since childhood: the dance teacher; the college theater professor; Happy, the locally famous TV clown with a raging alcohol addiction and an affinity for little girls (though not, apparently, their guinea pigs, which my mother learned the hard way). At thirty-six, divorced and childless, The Women are not pleased with me. They glimpse, on the horizon, their flickering flames.

Staring at the dark-haired neighbor sipping from her mug, with all this simmering violence in the air, I feel vibrational. The neighbor could be a witch, an oracle, the source of all that is good and evil. She is multiplying, after all. And with such sinister self-possession. The phrase "the invisible enemy" the politicians keep bandying about reminds me of witchcraft, invisible enemy #1, once blamed for all manner of illness and destruction since at least the early modern era. All our old magical thinking circles back again, patterning over history like a lullaby. And we love pattern, humans do, because pattern is structure amid chaos, and structure amid chaos provides a sense of control. Think religion, mythology, story. The usual balms.

But patterns also provide the framework for cognitive ecstasy, as in when everything seems to connect, but doesn't quite. There's still a deep sense of mystery, a problem we can't quite solve. We like this sensation. It is called wonder. It is simultaneously comforting and uncanny. It feeds on paradox and thrives in the in-between places. We feel it when the familiar goes suddenly strange, or the strange becomes suddenly familiar. It happens when beauty hikes up her skirt to reveal the dagger strapped to her thigh. It's the recognition of something just outside our comprehension, a new connective thread still dangling in the wind. I feel I am at the epicenter of wonder these days, struck between fear of my lover and desire for him; fear of the outside world and an overwhelming nostalgia for what was; anticipation for a new life and still mourning the old one I left two years ago in Vermont with my ex-husband. Like a spider lost in her own web.

Watching the witch, I try to imagine the wonder of beholding your own child. The ultimate terror and awe. *Here*, I would say to The Women, holding up our perfect mandala, *I made her for you*.

*   *   *   *   *

I used to mitigate my desire to have a baby by writing, but sometime in my midthirties it stopped working. My only sibling, my younger brother, Eric, kept overdosing on heroin, and because I could not save his life I felt the longing to create one even more acutely. Making *something* felt like the only way to counteract the unmaking of his slow death. I wrote and wrote, but I wasn't writing fast enough to fill the hole that his death would create. If I worked hard enough, I reasoned, I could counter death's pull with its antithesis. A life force to outweigh the death force. For all the years I was with the husband, my every day was a kind of hedging of bets, a tidying of loose ends, as if a marriage and a child and a house in Vermont and a tenure-track job would save me (and everyone I loved, *magically!*) from dying. It was this anticipatory grief, this wonder, through which I most often staggered and raged. In other words, his imminent death fueled me.

But a marriage and a child and a house in Vermont and a tenure-track job are only signs of privilege—like this book and the luxury to consider childbearing a choice—and death doesn't give a fuck about my privileges. And anyway, books would not sate The Women so much as a child. I thought about a friend whose aunt had died a week before the friend's baby was born. She and her partner named the baby after the aunt. The baby was not the aunt, but she was something. At the funeral, my friend's mother held the newborn tightly and rocked while the rabbi prayed. Watching her, I thought, art is not real in the way a child is real.

We cannot cradle art in our arms or cover it in kisses, or if we do, it will not kiss us back. The abstraction of art-making cannot compare to the irrefutability of a body inside a body, or a body in flames. Art is like prayer. But what we pray for are our people.

* * * * *

I realize the error in this logic—life is not the antidote to death. One life does not replace another. But never confuse logic for truth.

* * * * *

So, what *is* the solution to death, then?

The Women will not say. They can't explain it.

They want what's best for me, of course they do.

* * * * *

We were eighteen when the husband and I met, kids ourselves. My father had been dead six months, having fallen, drunk, down a flight of stairs. After a while, Jack's body became an extension of my body. I did not know where my body ended and his began. We graduated from college and then proceeded to grow up together, lockstep, like little boppity boy and girl dolls. *Boop bop*, off we went. He plugged my holes, so to speak, and me his. When I forgot, he remembered. Where I was loud, he was quiet. I broke things and he fixed them. He resented and I loved. I cooked and he ate. When I flailed, he was the tether. In those days I was always just about to lose my shit. I got lost constantly. I worked late and forgot to call. Every time Eric relapsed, I despaired. Once, I spilled soup on Leonardo DiCaprio while working at a fancy restaurant in New York and cried on the apartment floor for two days. Once, I did cocaine with the regulars and went home at dawn in another woman's dress. Once, I made out with the prep cook inside the meat freezer and never told Jack. I insisted we move again and again, state to state, as I impulsively chased jobs, writing classes, more "aesthetically conducive landscapes" (my words, *dear god*) in which to write. I wrote feverishly and waited tables while Jack found full-time, grownup work and largely supported us. Those were my salad days. He did not salad. We were twenty, twenty-three, twenty-five. I was not quirky or witty or waifish like the white leads performing their salad days in romcoms from the nineties. There really is nothing charming about a woman acting out her deepest fears, though whole narrative tropes try to convince us otherwise: the damsel in distress, the crazy girlfriend, the witchy bookworm cum sexpot who rejects your advances but eventually gives it up. This is not one of those stories. This is vaudeville, baby. This is a charade.

*　*　*　*　*

Here he is now, an adult-sized mirage, my brother knocking on the guest-room door and nine months sober, his longest stretch of sobriety since he was thirteen years old. We're in our midthirties, staying with our mother for the first time in nearly two decades, and regressing by the day. Two nights ago, we fought over which movie to watch. Yesterday, it was who did the dishes last. This morning, he tried to say he hadn't left a *giant shit* to fester in the toilet like roadkill. His girlfriend is pregnant and he needs to use my SUV for his new landscaping business, the one he hasn't started yet because he's never landscaped a day in his life. "But I'm watching YouTube videos about it," he says. "You think I can haul a lawnmower on the bus? Come on." For years he'd feared he was, ya know, "shooting blanks" because "there were so many times ladies coulda gotten knocked up" but didn't. This upset him. He wanted to be a father. He wanted that more than anything. I'd had no idea; we'd never talked about it. I'd been so busy worrying his sobriety, trying to solve it like some puzzle that only required the right combination of words, deeds, and financial assistance programs, I'd failed to consider he might have a sense of self outside of his addiction. Desires and interests beyond the ken of drugs. A vested interest in military history, maybe. Lesser-known Marley tracks. Grandma porn. Irrigation systems for premium cultivation of all four thousand potato varieties in Peru. How would I know? I'd never asked. (I did, however, once glimpse some grandma porn on his cell phone, so I wasn't completely ignorant.) All we ever talked about—on those rare occasions between relapses—existed inside a six-inch, six-day radius. His jail sentence; his commissary needs; the new guy at the halfway house; the various effects of prescription cocktails that changed by the day and doctor; and of course, a litany of logistics and urgent requests. Money, rides, his ever-vanishing ID cards, clothes, a new cell phone. He'll be a father in a month.

"You'll need a website," I tell him, putting down my book. I close the curtain on the neighbor and follow him down the stairs and outside. "You'll need a website and a Facebook ad and an Instagram account. You can do Mom's yard first and post before and after pics."

"A what account?" he says.

The one-eyed dog giveth not a fuck. He's reappeared beneath the crabapple tree, asleep again and bounding across invisible plains. He would like, perhaps, a bit of something sweet later, or if he's feeling decadent, a bloody tampon from the trash can. He humbles me daily. Like the rest of us, he's only living out the nature of his conditions. I think he prefers the liminal space of dreams for this reason, where these conditions—dog; grass; rabbit—send him soaring through the air instead of limping painfully into a heap. It occurs to me that this virus, too, is only behaving according to the conditions through which it exists, here on earth, and not through the anthropomorphized hungers we've ascribed to it.

We sit in the sun while he smokes. "An Instagram account," I say, pulling it up on my phone and noticing that no one has liked my story.

"Great. You know how to make one of those, right?"

I take quick drags from his cigarette so that they don't count, having quit again a year ago. Last week, he was laid off from his job as a waiter, the only work he can get with a couple of felonies. The restaurant is closed indefinitely. So is the rest of the world. The landscaping business is a good idea, despite his lack of actual experience and know-how. He figures people will want their yards prepped for spring; the garden beds cleaned, weeded, and mulched; old leaves raked and bagged; their lawns mowed. After all, we're spending a lot of time at home. There is a whole demographic right here in our mother's neighborhood who can't afford professional landscaping, per se, but might be willing to pay for the prep. He can do that. How hard can it be? He'll buy some used equipment off Craigslist, make a website, print up some fliers. He takes a last drag and then stands. In a few weeks he'll have enough money to buy a beater truck and haul the shit himself. Never mind that he won't have his license back until he's *like eighty*.

He stubs out his cigarette. The dog paddles nowhere. I agree to take him into the city to meet a guy from Craigslist who's selling an old lawnmower. As we speed down the empty turnpike, he leans over the screen of his phone, dripping sweat that he wipes fastidiously with the napkins he keeps in his pocket for this purpose. Another side effect of the medications that help keep him sober: Suboxone, Wellbutrin, others I can't recall. The sweating embarrasses him, and he wipes the napkin across his pale forehead and over the top his head, his hair balding and close-cropped, but swept to the side to appear fuller.

"Is this better?" he asks me timidly, smoothing the hair to the left. I glance at him in the passenger seat. His face is gleaming and pock-marked, puffy and dark around the eyes. Three teeth are missing, and another one will abscond before I return to Columbus. He looks like a child and an elderly man at the same time, sickly and infantile, more side effects of the medications. Prior to the job at the Broad Axe, he'd lost another restaurant job because customers had complained about the sweating. The manager had called him into his office after his shift. One lady claimed his sweat had landed in her soup. He did not argue with the manager. He did not explain. Quietly, he took off his apron, collected his tips, and called his mother to pick him up. He waited for her on the curb, squinting while taking long drags on a cigarette, and watching the soup lady struggle to unlock her Cadillac.

"Hey, good luck, man," Robbie called from the door of the restaurant, his apron untied. "Yo, mind if I bum a smoke?"

Beside me in the car, he waits for my approval. "Much better," I say. "Very handsome."

He sighs and fiddles with the radio, then returns his attention to the screen. He's trying to figure out how to set up a Venmo account, which I told him he'd need if he wanted an easy, no-contact way for customers to pay him. His relationship with technology is strained. He can't keep up while he's using or in jail, and he often can't afford it during his brief periods of sobriety, so for the short time that he's able to hold on to a phone (his Obama-phones, as he calls them), he is as obsessive about it as the boy who once played Nintendo for so many hours in a row that he couldn't move his neck for a week. I can still see his little blue moon face rapt in its glow. Now he can't get past the most rudimentary of functions: phone calls, texts, and nineties-style games like poker and Mario Brothers. The lag in his real-world experience reminds me how much of his life has been spent in absentia, like a man in and out of a coma.

*   *   *   *   *

In high school, we had one class together, Computer Basics, when I was a senior and he was a freshman. We learned Microsoft Office applications like Word and Excel and in this arena alone he surpassed me academically. I had been a classic over-achiever, my self-worth entirely dependent upon good grades and praise from grownups. Eric had been the opposite, plagued by ADHD, or at least its diagnosis, and even at thirteen an avid pot smoker and slacker. But when it came to computers, he was a natural, and completed the in-class assignments easily and quickly before emailing me the answers from the back row of the computer lab. When the teacher caught on to our scheme a few weeks into the quarter, she was outraged, pulling us out of the classroom to confront us with our identical assignments. We tried to feign remorse, but couldn't hide our grins as she dialed our mother.

"I'm sorry. You said *Jess* cheated off of *Eric*?" we heard our mother say. We laughed then, we couldn't help it, hearing our mother laughing over the phone, all while our poor, chagrined teacher sputtered admonishments to no one in particular.

"Don't ever do that again," our mother reprimanded us that evening over dinner at a diner, the three of us cackling like hens.

*   *   *   *   *

"You know who knows how to landscape?" Eric says when we get back with the lawnmower. "Dads," he says grinning.

Later, he pushes an imaginary stroller across the street, looking both ways with an exaggerated sense of concern. "You know who pushes strollers?" he says. "Dads."

It's his new and constant refrain. I follow him around giggling like a groupie. Everything he does is a marker of his impending fatherhood, ever more remarkable and darkly funny because so many of these activities are merely *stuff that adults do*. Adults who haven't spent the last twenty years addicted to heroin, anyway. Cooking, going to the doctor, opening a bank account. Submitting half their waking hours to the mind-suck of their phones.

Once, the three of us had been a front against our father's unending crises, precursors to his death from addiction when we were teenagers: drunken car accidents, arrests, belligerent phone calls, emergency room visits. Then, we had been a team. A gaggle. A comedy of errors. Our mother burned chickens and we drove my first car backward through the neighborhood, laughing when I hit a mailbox. Now, roles have shifted, and we are all a little fatter. I work too much and yell at everyone to be quiet. I cook elaborate meals no one appreciates. We forbid our mother from seeing her friends because *it's a goddamn pandemic*. She sneaks hits from her bowl in the garage and sleeps until eleven.

Meanwhile, dads like my brother get up early and go to work. Dads grill burgers. Dads fall asleep on the couch at nine. Dads take their meds and keep their shit together because that's what dads do.

Not ours, of course, but other dads.

* * * * *

When I was a kid, I watched The Women compulsively. I studied my mother smoking like some people watch their mothers cooking or applying makeup. She smoked angrily like women on TV kissed their no-good lovers. Or she smoked joyfully as if releasing a string of birthday balloons. I watched Mommom wipe crumbs from Poppop's mouth. I watched her worry her husband's dementia and then scuffle off to work. The Women knew how to *work*. Sold real estate, both of them, as a team. They worked all of the time. They were very good at working and proud of it too. Growing up, I saw their working as the highest ideal of womanhood, the most moral and essential. While the women worked, Poppop dozed on the sofa, my father drank in motel rooms, and my brother and I ate buttered matzo for dinner. These were our conditions. Women worked; men languished. That's just how it was. When they weren't working, I watched The Women walking and sleeping and driving and picking food from their teeth. I listened to them talk. I absorbed their cadences and rhythms, and the ways they related to one another— Mommom bossy and precise; my mother simultaneously defensive and appeasing. We never knew when my father, who usually stayed away during his benders, was going to land in jail or show up at the door, so it felt especially important that I stay attuned to The Women for clues. Watching them helped me figure out what was going on and how to prepare. When my mother began chain-smoking, it was an indication that she knew more about his condition than she was letting on. When The Women whispered, I could count on a sudden trip to the beach for a few days, my grandparents, my mom, Eric, and me, and an extended absence from school. It meant my father was "on the loose" after absconding from rehab, say, turning up only to self-flagellate on our front lawn. (Yes, of course I recognized the pattern, all those years later, watching my lover doing the same.) Shit could hit the fan at any moment; it was easier when I knew it was coming. Watching helped me shape chaos into pattern. In this way, watching The Women was a form of resilience, one my brother never developed. Recently, when I was still in Columbus, I realized that I still listen for subtle clues in my mother's tone when I answer her calls. They indicate whether my brother is sober or using, alive or dead. As if by "figuring it out" before she tells me will soften the blow. Or when I'm home visiting, like now, I listen to my mother on the phone and try to guess, from context clues and the manner of her speech, who she is talking to and what they are talking about. I'm almost always right.

When we were girls, my best friend, Jessie, and I would listen to her on the phone using her "work voice," then playact the voice back to one another, taking turns being the client or the realtor. Jessie was best at it. As it turns out, she went into the family business. They work in the same office. She pleases my mother in ways that I can't. When I visit them in the office, Jessie sounds exactly like her. "Thanks, Bob, for sending over the paperwork," I hear her say in that pseudo-sophisticated way, "I'll get back to you shortly. Uh-huh. Uh-huh. Uh-huh. Right, Bob. Great. Will do. Buh-bye." She holds up her finger to me through her office window and I flash her my boobs. She has a lot of nerve. "Don't you finger me," I mouth, to which she shows me a different finger. She is my other woman, the one with whom all the growing and suffering and fucking up has gone down.

"I love you," I tell her later as I'm leaving the office, pulling keys from my bag.

"You'll do," she says, and hugs me good and long.

*   *   *   *   *

Nobody wants to read about babies. For one, they rarely say anything provocative. Also, their worldview is too messy, antithetical to the purposes of literature. I watch Jessie with her baby, Jules, on FaceTime. Jules smacks Jessie's face then runs to her bookshelf. "Do you want to read a book?" Jessie says. The baby pauses and cocks her head to the side. No, she does not want to read a book. She does not believe reading a book will be an edifying experience. All the world is an infringement on her autonomy right now, including her pleading mother. "No," says Jules, tossing a book to the floor. "No," she says, flinging another. "No, no, no, no," the books flying from their place on the shelf, punctuating her siren song. Her fat, little arms spin like a softball pitcher's. "Ah," I scream. "Make it stop!"

Baby transgressions are not provocative in the way that adult transgressions are provocative. There is no logic or plan behind Jules's insurrection. Babies don't have motives, they have impulses, subject only to the body's whims. In this way, they are not so different from my father, for one, who, helpless to these whims, could not keep his own body alive. Some days I think, why would I willingly introduce the chaos of a child into a life spent fleeing it? Babies are tyrants. They impose an order of their own divining. They care nothing for your survival except that it ensures their own. If writing is an attempt to control the world around us, to bend it to our will, then making babies is the exact opposite. To supplicate oneself to this nonsensical regime would be, I imagine, true surrender.

Humans desire connection above all else: to see a body in the landscape and the landscape in a body. Of course, I want a body from my body. A daughter to be my mother's granddaughter. Pattern keeps us sane.

Or, as Timothy Leary said, "To use your head you must go out of your mind."

*   *   *   *   *

Jack left me three years ago. We were thirty-three and two years into our marriage, and in those early days of his leaving I went into shock. I mean, I could not move my body. I felt like a toddler forever frozen in the moment between falling to the ground and deciding whether the ordeal warranted a scene. I sat on the living room floor in our empty house on a hill in Vermont, gapemouthed and snotty. Everything I knew to be true was no longer true. It was a wonder, an astonishment, by which I mean the language it had taken us fifteen years to invent was suddenly dead.

We were the only people on the planet who knew its syntax and silent glances; its jokes and gestures; its noises and nonverbal indicators. It would never be spoken again. I hadn't seen it coming and yet I had always seen it coming. When it became hard to swallow the wine, I knew I was in trouble.

Two practices saved me. The first was looking at the paintings of Mary Pratt. I had a coffee-table book of Pratt's paintings that I'd take to bed with me. They were my first visions in the morning and the last before bed. Pratt was Canadian, a homemaker in the fifties and sixties, and for a long time she put off painting to support her husband and raise their four children. But one day while mopping she was struck by a strip of light across an unmade bed. The charge she felt was erotic. When I read that in a 2015 interview, the year my marriage began and subsequently began to unravel, I knew exactly what she meant. Women have always known the beauty of the quotidian. Not just domestic landscapes, but the rhythms of their daily makings and unmakings. I felt that erotic charge when I looked at her paintings, too, scenes from her domestic life: a severed fish head in the sink; jars of cooling red jelly; a plate of mangoes. In their sumptuousness and clarity of vision, they divined in me a new way of seeing. It felt holy, this seeing, or revolutionary. I could not decide. Perhaps the pain made this new vision possible. I felt those early days of separation as if I were living inside a silver tunnel of despair. It was sharp, bright, and utterly consuming. The world did not go dull, as some have described depression, but as if tuned to an unbearable decibel. This was wonder too, I realized later, the whole known world gone strange.

The walking, then, for hours every day through the Vermont winter, my second practice of salvation, eased the splitting sensory overload. I could channel pain into movement. I could outrun it. I looked for the divine in the flotsam alongside the road; Pratt's fish heads and eggshells. The wind winked. The rye grass seethed. Out of my grief grew a hot shoot of desire. I wanted to fuck every person I passed on these walks, a reminder that I was still alive. The one-eyed dog was irreverent. He took off into the snowy hills and returned bearing the bloody carcasses of field mice, proud as a teenager with a bag of mediocre pot, as if he already knew what I was just discovering. Wonder was the sublime in the spiritual sense, wherein our deepest griefs and biggest pleasures together sear a hole into the psyche too deep to escape. Might as well embrace it.

*   *   *   *   *

Eric's landscaping business is called We Can Still Grow. I build him a simple website and he designs fliers that our mother and I distribute in neighborhood mailboxes during our daily walks with the one-eyed dog. People hesitate when they see us stuffing their mailboxes in our blue plastic gloves but they call. He studies YouTube videos to learn just how, exactly, one landscapes. We loan him money for a cheap tiller from Home Depot that takes us five days and two return trips to assemble. He is proud of himself and so are we. Elated. Our mother is practically giddy. She laughs and talks endlessly about her forthcoming granddaughter. I have never seen her so happy. While the world panics and grieves, my mother is all bliss. She laughs, she dances, we play endless games of poker. She has her two children and a grandchild on the way. It is all she has ever wanted, *her one true ambition*, as she told me long ago, and though she has suffered unfathomably for it, here we are. I am trying not to panic, but I can't help sensing this moment like the temporary bliss of the terminally ill, those who in their final hours inexplicably run smiling and naked down hospital corridors before just as suddenly lying down to die. Here we are summoning new life just as the world is taking its final bow. Or if we survive this pandemic, then what? Do I really believe my brother's decades of addiction are behind him? That he will be a good father to his daughter, having had no such model? That he won't abandon her as we were abandoned by our father? And even in the dark reaches of my brain, do I not question how it is that my brother—sick, inept, selfish, and so often mean—gets to have a child when I do not?

*　*　*　*　*

To his great shock, the business flourishes. His girlfriend holes up with her parents a few miles away and they make plans to get an apartment together after the baby is born. Sometimes I take my mother's car and drive by his jobsites just to glimpse him at work, his white T-shirt wet and dirt-slaked, while he digs and pulls and shapes the earth. And what work! I can't believe how he works. The visible, physical kind and whatever work keeps him sober. My brother, a father? Is this not a wonder too? He stops and takes a long pull of water, wipes his gloves on his jeans. How has he become this person I do not recognize, so wildly resilient, when only a year ago he was all submission?

It strikes me now that I have been writing about my brother for as long as I have been writing. It is an illusion of control, this writing, the same way he believes, right now, that the perfect mound of dirt he has sculpted around the base of that cherry tree will not erode beneath torrential rains, the creeping phlox will flower despite mosaic virus, that the wisp of girl-child, churning slowly now toward the sun, will flourish inside the eclipse of his absence.

*　*　*　*　*

Then one night at dinner, Eric is too tired to eat. He picks at my latest experiment, a curried chicken with peanuts and cilantro. His body hurts. His hands. We wait on him like nursemaids. Here, a water. Here, another napkin. Here, some Tylenol. Our mother fetches him a heating pad for his aching back.

"I'm the one who cooked the goddamn dinner," I say to the one-eyed dog.

Dads, he reminds us, need rest, and the traitorous beast curls beside his feet.

In the morning, it begins. We drive him to the hospital to join his girlfriend. Her parents drop her off at the front door and we let Eric off a few hundred yards behind. They stand beside their car in masks, hug their daughter, wave to us, and then leave. We watch Eric walk slowly toward his girlfriend and the hospital doors. Toward the rest of his life. Nobody else is allowed to join them because of COVID, so we go home and wait by our phones.

Around noon, I start dozing on the sofa, only to scream awake ten minutes later when the phone rings—*I've been preselected for a new credit card!* On the muted television a woman is weeping. There's a shot of a swaddled patient hooked up to a ventilator, then the image switches to an elderly man pressing his hand against a window. On the right of the screen death tolls continue climbing. It could be the stock market, the lottery jackpot. None of it makes sense. My mother pirouettes through the living room carrying a glass of iced tea. Her phone rings and I sit up. It's her best friend. They titter in excitement as she paces into the kitchen. I text Jessie: "Any minute now!" But she doesn't reply. She's one of the few people in her office still required to come in so she's busy constructing a shield out of polypropylene and dirty looks. She sends me a selfie wearing three masks, plastic glasses, and gloves. At home, her husband waits anxiously with their two-year-old. They'd both been violently sick last week and there were a couple days of panic while they waited for his COVID test results. Turns out the husband and the kid had eaten some bad pears that were later recalled, but that pocket of time between knowing and not-knowing was, for Jessie, a screaming black hole.

My mother comes back from the kitchen and sits down beside me on the couch. She's gripping her phone and grinning, and with her other hand she reaches over and squeezes my shoulder. The one-eyed dog circles, then spots the orange cat in the corner and gives chase. The cat darts, then turns around and slaps him across the face. I pick up *Philadelphia Magazine* and flip through a feature about up-and-coming restaurants nobody will be eating at; read an article about summer concerts nobody will attend. In one photo, a lawn is covered in blankets and people. The people are smiling, clapping, drinking, wrapping their arms around one another and singing. A tiny boy is sitting on a red-striped beach ball holding a taco, maybe, or a sandwich. A group of young girls are draped over one another atop a purple blanket, their mouths open in muted chorus. A couple kisses. A child does a headstand. One guy looks incredibly bored.

My mother puts the phone on the coffee table in front of us and we stare at it—tiny oracle of doom and light—and wait for it to ring. We wait for a long time.

It is April 21, 2020.

* * * * *

I was thirty-one when I started this book. Jack had just confessed that he didn't want to have children. Not with me, or anyone, ever. We were newly engaged. I did not know what to do, so I did what I knew how to do. I thought maybe I could write my way through big questions about the nature of creation. I thought I could discover something grand and unifying, something essential about what it means to be a woman, an artist, and a mother. Could I make art instead of children? Would that satisfy the creative imperative I felt beating itself out inside me like a wild hare? And what of the choke of death? How could I be a woman, an artist, and a mother under the specter of my brother's imminent death? With what fortitude? What feral instinct? Why did I get to live this life while he merely suffered it?

I did not find those answers in this book.

During the long, dark hours of my divorce, a couple years after Jack's confession, I looked at one painting by Mary Pratt more than the others. *Service Station* (1978). I crossed it like an ocean, caressed it like a lover. It made me angry in ways I could not articulate. While much of Pratt's work, however lauded, has come to represent the supposed quiet steadiness of a woman's domestic life (as if such a thing exists!), there are darker undercurrents. It is not the sumptuousness of the chocolate cake that impresses me, but the salient edge of the silver blade beside it (*Chocolate Birthday Cake*, 1997). It is not the simplicity and directness of *Eggs in an Egg Crate* (1975), nor even the radiant light and translucency that Pratt creates, but the striking emptiness of those six jagged, broken shells that compel me, their delicate insides spilling out like so much spent fertility. Here is someone who knows something about what it means to be a woman, an artist, and a mother. This is how the essayist works, too, by studying experience with relentless precision to reveal the irresolvable, contradictory, beautiful, terrible truths therein. We are like surgeons this way. We watch and study and slice the world open. We finger its ridges until it splinters and spills. In *Service Station* (1978), a flayed moose carcass hangs suspended by the truss of a flatbed truck. The light is a sickly green and the carcass is an empty coat of glistening muscle and wet, curving ribs. The hooves are spread wide and pointed to the ceiling. There is no doubt that the image is violent, ferocious, feminine. Blood splatters the cardboard scattered across the floor and smears the truck's bumper. The source images came from her friend Ed Williams, a mechanic in Salmonier, Canada. The images he gave her initially confounded Pratt. She held on to them for years before making the painting. In that time, her infant son died when only a day old, preceded by his twin while still in the womb. Her son John suffered a brief but harrowing brush with cancer. "I got through that, and then I said to myself: you can do this now," Pratt said, referencing the image of the splayed moose. "You know what this is about."

My life changed drastically between when I started this book and ended it. Not just my personal life but everything. The world grew hotter and caught fire. A pandemic decimated the population. A million horrors befell us. A million mitzvahs too. Tides have dressed and undressed our shores over and again. I adapted, revised, rewrote. At one point, I realized I no longer knew what the book was about. The composition was all wrong. I nearly tossed it.

I envied Pratt's certainty. This was the source of my defeat: I never knew what any book I wrote was "about." The question always befuddled me. How was I to take this great swath of experience, ideas, feelings, and forms only to pluck out a few choice words and say, *this*, this is what this book is about? As if we could say the same of a life. I could not, finally, declare big truths, even though I felt them in my body—strokes of light where once there beat a heart. But what if the creative imperative is not about creating anything, but instead beckoning forth what's already there? Breaking open our brittle chests to lay hands on the wreckage, tender the red, wet wound?

Essayist Mary Cappello writes, "Instead of writing *about*, as in 'what is your book about?,' [creative nonfiction] writes *from*. Or nearby or toward, under, around, through, and so on." I think she means we need more specific verbs with which to calculate the problems of language and love.

This is a book from wonder. It is a book amid women; inside anticipatory grief; through our mothers; and toward something substantial. This is one book under love. It is in pursuit of the creative imperative. When Pratt's old friend Ed Williams finally saw the painting that had taken her so many years to make, he studied it for a long time, shook his head, grinned, and said, "Well, well. There's my old truck." I laughed when I read that. Because of course, of all the things the painting is about, it's also about that (or through, or aside, or against), everything it conjures in the viewer. The meaning is a third space over which neither the maker nor the beholder has complete dominion. It's in the collision of their distinct perceptions. The center of a Venn diagram. Its own thing. It is as much a painting about Ed Williams's old truck (and everything that image evokes in him) as it is about anything else—Pratt's tremulous grief, for instance. Love is discourse. It is relational. Maybe this is why we persist in pouring love into third spaces: children, art, intoxicants like sex and drugs. It's only there that it seems to make any sense. There, outside the self. There, where we can look at it together and marvel, our twined love mixing together and apart like paint in a bucket of water. Like a pattern that won't keep still, refuses to be solved, but holds us rapt anyway. Like a witch's gaze. Like a new spring, letting down her hair. Like the splayed ribs of a dead moose. Like your old truck.

—MAY 14, 2021

[IN THE BEGINNING]

In the beginning, in our original unwoundedness ("innocence"),
we live in an unconscious but real state of full connection. . . .
But, I am afraid, we must "leave the garden"; and usually
around the age of seven, we increasingly "think" of ourselves
as separate. . . . This is the essential illusion that spirituality
seeks to overcome: "How do I get back to the garden of union and
innocence?" Objectively I have never left, but it feels like I have.
—RICHARD ROHR, from "Homecoming"

In the beginning, there is one woman. She is light and dark and
warm and humming and I do not know where her body ends
and mine begins. It is the spring of 1984, just northwest of Philadelphia in a suburb called Conshohocken, fifteen minutes from
where the woman was born and grew up rebellious and bored.
Outside the dark and smoky apartment everything is blooming.
The whole world is going to space. The apartment is on the third
floor and it is one of thirty-seven other apartments just like it,
brown and boxy. There is a willow tree in the window and a television always tuned to soap operas or the news. *Challenger* takes
off with Sally Ride inside, who recently became the first American woman in space. Beside her is Kathryn Sullivan, soon to become the first American woman to walk in space. The woman,
a new mother, watches space on the television screen, the child
in her arms, just like she'll watch two years later when the *Challenger* explodes, killing two different women: Judith Resnik,

smart and Jewish like her, and the beloved, fair-haired teacher from New Hampshire, Christa McAuliffe. The woman watches women fly and fall, fly and fall. It's the eighties. Before the child, she'd been spaced out, orbiting aimlessly. Motherhood was the spaceship she'd thought would gentle her back to earth. Though she won't admit it to the child for nearly forty years, she'd had to beg the man to marry her. It was their fourth pregnancy together and this time she wasn't letting anyone take it away. Except now she is sinking under the weight of her own determination. She feels extraneous, outsized, alone, tired, and desperately lucky. Love has physical form. The woman's big love is now externalized. She is happy. Her love is visible, validated, although somehow still grotesque. Oh, well.

We are onebody. We laugh and the woman traces circles on my face and we sleep.

Watch.

A woman and an infant. Soon a tiny, tipsy towhead who is one, then two years old. This is pre-language, so sights are sounds are smells are the sponge of the mother's skin. The dark apartment thrums, not unlike the womb. This is the whole universe: the dark apartment, our body, constellations of light and dark, a whirling cosmos, *what else?* Wet, weighted air. Smoke. The sensation of floating from room to room.

Every day, her parents, the same parents who had so ardently refused to support her during her pregnancy, arrive at the apartment, brush past her, and scoop up the child. She had, after all, married the child's father just weeks before giving birth, in a small courthouse ceremony, wearing an off-white polyester shift dress and sensible shoes. For their honeymoon, the couple had spent the weekend in the Poconos, during which her new husband got drunk nightly and insisted they dance to the songs he requested of the resort's house band, his mustache damp and itchy on her neck.

Now the woman eats soft things and looks out the window at the parking lot and hums. The child's father, mercifully, is gone all day, then comes home smelling of oil and beer and shedding asbestos dust from his work clothes like snow. Her hair, once a plume of curls and Aqua Net, weighs heavy on her head like a dozing cat. Only a year ago, she'd traipsed off to New York City with her friend Karen, a fellow theater graduate from Temple, intent on a life of drama and stardom. She'd lasted a week before slinking back to Philadelphia, crestfallen and broke, her father glib. Her parents had refused to help her, emotionally or financially, and she'd quickly grown scared, in over her head. She rocks the child day and night, dozing, nursing, smoking, while Karen moons seductively on the soap opera *Dynasty*, her blonde hair tended like precious silk.

Some days when the man comes home, they go to parties and drink vodka and snort speed and watch the baby in her bassinet who, everyone agrees, is *good, so good, what a good baby, have you ever seen such a good baby, just look at her, who's she look like ya think? Wow, so good.*

Some days when the man comes home, she sends him back out for cigarettes and diapers.

Some days when the man comes home, they eat ground beef smothered in cream of mushroom soup in front of the television while the baby sleeps on her lap.

Some days when the man comes home, they fight and count change on the carpet until they have enough for formula and a frozen chicken pot pie from ShopRite.

The man comes home and comes home and comes home and then he doesn't come home. Oh, well.

* * * * *

Before long, I grow larger. I sit up. I learn to chew, walk, repeat words, and turn doorknobs. We flee the apartment and the man. We read stories about birds, apples, women. Stories are tangible. There is no difference—in this beginning—between the physical world and my imagination. Stories comprise a larger body into which we fit perfectly. We are safe here, held, and this body is feminine because I do not know another kind of body. Her cigarette smoke curls around us, but even the smoke is not separate but extensions of the sounds we make. There is the woman, stories, love, and me, and together we are one aggregate form.

But then the man returns and shortly thereafter a boy-child appears. This is a great shock. The man and the boy-child, I know intuitively, are not part of the constellation that is my whole world. And now the boy-child does not know where his body ends and hers begin. We cleave then, the first woman and me, and our one body becomes two separate bodies. I do not understand that the cleaving has been happening all along. I do not know what love is beyond the purview of our onebody.

Onebody. What I mean is that when the infant cleaves from her mother, a wound is created that she will spend a lifetime trying to fill. Their flesh history is slowly erased, swallowed by a black hole of forgetting. Society demands it. Watching it go, the mother grieves and gasps. It is wounding, but also a wonder to watch herself slowly detach from herself, like a satellite released into orbit.

Wonder, which derives from the Old English *wundor*, which may be cognate not only with the German *wunder* but also with *wunde*: cut, gash, *wound*. Wonder also means "something that causes astonishment." So, our first wound is also our first wonder. We are astonished by our cleaving. *Attonitus* in Latin: thunderstruck. We are thunderstruck by the cleaving. I do not yet know that cleaving of one sort or another will happen again and again in this life, that pain is central to love. That neither can be experienced without the other. There is so much to learn.

My only comfort is when she reads me stories before bed. She holds me in her lap and I listen to her voice, smell her skin, and pretend we are onebody again. When she doesn't read me stories before bed—when she is too tired, or angry, or desirous to be elsewhere (because she is still a woman who desires, after all)—I cry myself to sleep. Her independent desires, I intuit, reinforce our separation. They show me again and again that I am *not-her*, though I was once. Now I know that misunderstanding my mother's desires was my first failure as her daughter. I carry the cleaving like a birthmark, a kiss of psychic hurt. It is not a trauma; only the ordinary extraordinary pain of being human. We all bear it. We all, as Franciscan friar Richard Rohr puts it, spend a lifetime trying to return to "the garden of union and innocence." The lushness of that first landscape cast off to distant horizons. There go I, human girl-child, to forever chase this verdant mirage.

It doesn't help that the father is a drunk and the boy-child a prolific crier. I watch from the carpet, the bedroom, the tub, the car seat. She wrestles them both, the man and the boy-child, the big one always coming, going, tripping, and passing out in his boots; the little one an angry, wailing miniature god. She sits on the couch all night long holding him to her breast, dozing and lurching awake, then smoking and stroking his wet cheeks. I am four, five, then six years old. I am learning that women are forms designed to control the chaos of men, and this idea will be reinforced again and again in my life, orienting me toward the women in whose orbits I could feel safe. This is the story I tell myself about myself, and like any story, it circles back again and again to the beginning.

[HALF WOMAN, HALF WONDER]

She must have wanted this, this predicament, these
contradictions. She believes physical conception must
be "enabled" by will or desire, like any other creative act.
—SUSAN HILLER

I spent the impetuousness of my twenties in love. In love with a
man, sure, but also in love with a woman named Rosie, my boss
at the Italian restaurant, who taught me how to present a bottle
of wine like a goddamn boss. In love with my elderly landlords,
war survivors, who showed me how loud love can be, and how
to weave story out of the scraps of love. In love with a small boy
I used to nanny, who was happiest with his head on my stomach and his thumb in his mouth. His soft, infant face churned
reflexively, eyes half-mast, as if born back into the fabric of the
Universe. In love with Mara from Italy who wet her pants when
she was excited and kissed me on the lips and took me to meet
her cousins—brawny, tender boys with whom I also fell in
love. They drove us to a sulfurous river near Siena and we swam
and smoked joints and I watched the water split around their
smooth waists. I was twenty-two: half woman, half wonder.

Years later, I met Mara in Philadelphia for dinner. She'd recently
moved to my hometown for graduate school and I was visiting
my mother from New York. We brought along our partners, men

we'd each been seeing for years. It's possible we had secret, naive plans for a foursome, Mara and me, but I can't remember. In Italy, three years prior, we'd made out in the bars and streets and once—as if playing roles in the movie version of our lives—in a gondola. We were college students then, studying art history in an international program. She was big and sensual. Had we been older, or less wounded in our bodies, we might have expressed our love better. I might have let my hands travel over her collarbone and under the sides of her shirt or pressed my body to her body, which is what I'd wanted but couldn't say. It was all I could do not to cry upon waking all those blue and tepid Italian mornings, tangled in the white, polyester curtains that flanked the window in my dorm room, against which my single cot was pressed.

Nights, we walked into the heart of Siena and sat on the cool stone of the central Piazza del Campo with all the other young people, drinking wine out of paper cups. Every half hour or so, we'd saunter into a bar, past the sneering men who dominated the stools, and into the bathroom to crush and snort her Ritalin until our nostrils burned a brilliant blue. The amphetamine cooled our emotions and lit our brains. We talked for hours. In the mornings, we ate pastries and drank coffee until about noon, when we could finally empty our bodies of the drugs and wine. In the afternoons, we stalked the winding streets of the city. I had no language for the newness of that old world. I was stunned silent and gaping. How many times we went into the cool dark of the Basilica of San Domenico I don't know; staring at the severed, mummified head of Saint Catherine who as a teenager cut off her hair and scalded herself to keep her family from forcing her into marriage. She joined a nunnery, made a vow of chastity, and married Jesus, who wrapped his sacred foreskin around her finger in lieu of a wedding band. From her spot inside the golden reliquary, she was always just about to speak, mouth open, eyes sewn shut.

———

In 1380, when she died at thirty-three, guards from Siena had to smuggle her head back from Rome, where she'd been living— her whole body would have been impossible to secret away— and still they were stopped at the border and searched. But Catherine's bagged head was no more than a pile of rose petals then, and only rematerialized after they'd safely returned to Siena.

Once, we stood before her for three hours without saying a word. We swayed on our skinny legs, a bag of pastry crumbs on the floor between us. Mara's uncle, who'd once pinched her soft, adolescent stomach while gingerly extracting a paper plate of birthday cake from her hands, had just died in a waterskiing accident and she was feeling particularly bummed. We had the notion that if we just waited long enough, Catherine would show us how to be women, so we waited and watched her, Mara and me, and I felt petals floating behind my ribs, stoking my lungs, but Catherine never said a word, never graced us with her benedictions—we shameful, foolish girls—who wanted so much and gave so little. We turned, and I took Mara's hand in mine before we walked down the aisle, breaking through scores of light streaming from the windows, and through the door. And even long after we had exited, turned right toward the duomo, and disappeared, Catherine sat silent and implacable as a corpse, which is, after all, what she is.

Whatever the attraction between us, we thought we needed the gaze of men to validate. So the day I left Italy, we unzipped and stepped out of love, as if tossing aside an ill-fitting party dress. We were smart, so how did we still not understand? Love does not just go away. Like all energy, it only morphs into something else.

*   *   *   *   *

When my father fell out of this world, I fell into it. This was five years before meeting Mara, April 2002. We were on our way to visit him at his mother's house, Eric and me, for the first time in a couple of years. He'd been promising us his sobriety, a new job, a home where we might be a family. This was not new and we were not convinced, but we agreed to visit. But before we could, late the night before, my father stood at the top of the attic staircase; his body seized and fell and stilled and left behind such stunning grief that for weeks I tottered through the house on autopilot, my mother's Ativan rattling in my pocket, wide-eyed and gob-smacked with love. "Hold on to these," she'd told me. "You'll need them." I was seventeen years old, six months from leaving home for good, and on that day, love left me thunderstruck.

And then I inherited his love. There were no forms or lawyers involved, but it was bequeathed. No doctors, but it was as literal as a heart transplant. I mean, his love left his body, traveled through the air, and entered my body. I saw it like I'd once watched Ghost Patrick Swayze enter Alive Demi Moore. His love smelled like Marlboros, Coors Lite, and spearmint gum. He died, and all that love didn't die, it only transformed. It grew large and graceless inside me like a golden retriever. In the beginning, all I could do was pace my grandmother's plush beige rooms. I walked into walls, turned, then shuffled off in the opposite direction like a hungry ghost. It was churning, his love; it was metastasizing.

* * * * *

Children of addicts learn how to love poorly. We lean toward love like windowsill plants toward a winter sun. The only love stories we know are rife with trouble. From my father, I saw that love for your family compels you to weep on the front lawn with your pants around your ankles, begging for forgiveness. Love urges you to swig vodka until you convulse wetly on the floor like a land-tossed fish. Love forces you to fuck the housewife next door for a couple of Klonopin. Leave the children unattended. Shatter trucks in the dull light of parking lot lampposts. Too much love will kill you, I intuited, and this was an acceptable or at least inevitable outcome.

So instead of letting it overtake me, I thought when I was a kid, it was prudent to manage love. I thought I better schedule it on the calendar, take down messages for love, dress it in tailored suits, sturdy pumps, and demand minutes by 4 p.m. This was the nineties after all, and so I also thought love could do anything with enough hairspray and chutzpah. Dolls were reprimanded rather than coddled; imaginary friends were women in power suits with 401ks and boundaries; and the protagonists in my stories always got their shit together when their spouses demanded it. But soon, I discovered that good grades and good-girl manners do not placate addiction, which I understood to be an excess of love—love's bottomless hunger—and so instead love made me want to hurt myself: punishment for all I had failed to understand.

The year I turned thirteen, I loved a boy named Derek so much I didn't consume more than five hundred calories a day for two years. I'd bite the inside of my cheeks until I bled; pinch my nipples with clothespins until they turned swollen and blue. If I ate an orange, I'd jump rope in the living room until my hips ached. I did sit-ups until I was sweating, watching the beautiful women dance on MTV, resplendent with love.

I was five foot eight and weighed eighty-seven pounds.
Love made me want to dissolve.

But then my father died and his love entered the ether and I was the nearest open wound. I did not dissolve, but all that extra love was as unwieldy as a third leg. I toddled with love. I lurched.

✳ ✳ ✳ ✳ ✳

After dinner that night in Philadelphia we returned to Mara's new apartment, tipsy and loud, and Jack and I followed her and her partner, whose name I have forgotten, up the narrow stairs of her building while a stream of urine bloomed down the back of her jeans. In her living room, we sat on a velvet couch while her partner quietly admonished her in the bedroom. What a thing, I marveled, for a body to express itself so literally. Also, what a relief it must be, to spill out of yourself. I was twenty-seven and hadn't yet had a proper orgasm. Love pushed at the boundaries of my body. To allow love to escape the safety of the body's form would have been dangerous (Mara; my father). So instead, I ached with love.

All night, I leaned into Jack. I studied his face for signs of emotion. If I loved like a slobbery dog, Jack had become my withholding trainer. He loved in redolent scraps plucked from a fanny pack. This was love measured and negotiated. I recognized the impulse. Sex, of course, earned me my keep. I learned to fake it, like so many women I knew. Jack hadn't been shown love as a child, not in the ways The Women had shown me love, loudly and affectionately. I wanted to teach him love like that, love that came when you called. Galloping love. Love that smelled like chewed leather and fresh meat. He liked when I laughed and when I left him alone. I became good at both. It seemed his hand was always reaching for that bag, so I waited, panting, ever the good girl.

We left at dawn while they slept, Jack and me, penning a note on the steamer trunk she used as a coffee table before skulking down the stairs to emerge into the suspended time of the city. It was foggy, cool, and quiet. I trailed Jack as he barreled forward, feeling like a fugitive from love, racing down the block toward his car. *Did I want to fuck the whole world?* I was a creep, gluttonous like my father. I knew it like I knew the damp hollows of my body then—naturally but at a distance.

I never saw Mara again.
It was no one's fault. It was one of those things.

*   *   *   *   *

And so I fell in love with strangers. With professors and baristas
and truck drivers and hotel clerks. Once, I fell in love with a cus-
tomer service representative in Iowa over the phone. I fell in love
with Annie Dillard and Raymond Carver and royal blue and my
own cunt. I fell in love with trash and wind and trailer parks nestled brightly on the beaches of Florida. I fell in love with Wim
Wenders and didn't leave the house for three days. I fell in love
with the blinding kitsch of America and stared full-faced, as
if at the sun. I fell in love with other people's children and the
holy mystery of the working miniature. (I think of my father
worrying his model sailboats in the evenings, their tiny masts
thin as toothpicks, the marvel of their stamp-sized sails catching his breath. Did he imagine himself an inch high, roaming
the planks, or instead the benevolent creator, omniscient and
good?) I fell for Renaissance art and Belgian beer. For churches
and drug addicts and mountains and the sensation of being
smacked across the face. I fell so hard for tomato juice one summer I drank until my gums bled. I ate raw kale until it burned.

*   *   *   *   *

Three months after publishing a book about my father, his life
and death, I received an email from a woman who claimed to
have had a relationship with him just prior to my birth, shortly
before he returned to my mother. I was skeptical until she sent
over a photo of a love letter he had written to her in his distinc-
tive slanting script, a cartoon sketch of Snoopy at the top calling out, "I LOVE YOU!" in huge rounded letters, the speech bubble so swollen it capsized over the edge of the page. He had been
twenty-five years old then. His love was so large all he could

manage was a single page-long run-on sentence enumerating the facets of his love, her attributes falling over one another like over-exuberant children, "articulate, sensitive, loving, just, fair, great in bed, great on the floor, great in the shower," and on and on and on, as if a love so magnanimous could only be expressed this way—by calling out its name. "There was something burning through him," she wrote in her email. "He was ALWAYS that person. Maybe he arose from the cradle already disassembling, I don't know."

The Bible says that Adam's first emotion was wonder. You can hear it in his initial words to Eve: "This at last is bone of my bones and flesh of my flesh." At last! In the 1600s the French philosopher René Descartes wrote, "When our first encounter with some object takes us by surprise, and we judge it to be new, or very different from what we have previously experienced or from what we expected it to be, this causes us to wonder at it and be astonished." Show my father a computer and his instinct was to take it apart, finger its wires and connections, the delicate ribs of its motherboard, struck with wonder. I once watched my father love a dog so hard, he trembled when she died. I watched him love so badly he stuck his whole tongue down the neck of an empty vodka bottle; licked it clean and dry. Descartes was familiar with extremes and cautioned against them: "Astonishment is an excess of wonderment that can only ever be bad." I believe that life suffused my father with such love and wonder that he froze in the face of it. He could break love down to its constituent parts, marvel at it, but he could not then put himself back together. He was as shattered as that motherboard.

* * * * *

Rapture of the deep, or nitrogen narcosis (also known as the Martini effect), is a condition that afflicts deep-sea divers, an anesthetic effect caused by a shift in gases at high pressure. At first, the effects are harmless—mild euphoria, a sense of "mastery over the environment." It's only when the diver goes deeper that the real danger arises—impaired judgment, loss of control and decision-making abilities. The lesson, the metaphor, is clear. Don't plumb the depths carelessly. Don't become reckless with love. The thing about metaphors, though, is not just their convenience. They are intrinsic to the way we move through the world. They come from the heavens and they come from the darkest reaches of the sea. They compose the invisible web of consciousness and art and obsession and love and wonder through which we make our way here on earth.

I'd first kissed Mara because her teeth were a marvel of design. I fell through a crack in a frozen lake because I couldn't stop myself from heaving ice chunks on ice floes, wondering at the shards of light. For more than a decade, I couldn't stand to live in the same place for longer than two years because the possibility of missing out on another shade of living was unbearable.

"The world is wilder than that in all directions," says my favorite essayist, Annie Dillard, "more dangerous and bitter, more extravagant and bright. We are making hay when we should be making whoopee; we are raising tomatoes when we should be raising Cain, or Lazarus." What to do with a love so unkempt and insatiable? So undisciplined it doesn't fit into the confines of a body, an essay, a lifetime? Is this God? Is it madness? The biologist Jeremy Griffith proffers that "people fall in love in order to abandon themselves to the dream of an ideal state (being one free of the human condition)." I'm drawn to this theory because it suggests that this love is larger than the vessel through which it operates. It reflects my sense that love must exist outside of the self, able to pass from one body to the next or get sliced open with a knife. We follow it toward wonder, that delicious, dangerous sensation—the conflation of terror and awe—which can lead us toward inquiry or away from it, toward discipleship. My father was a disciple of love, but also booze. Some people become disciples of religion, or yoga, or NASCAR. Anything to contain the uncontainable. A place to put our overwhelming love and fear. And should you bequeath such love to your next of kin, as we are wont to do, she should not shudder. She should not balk. She is only half a woman, after all.

Sometimes I'm afraid I will have a child simply to do it, because my body is capable of making a person and I can't fathom a lifetime of not experiencing an available experience. That there is no other vessel capacious enough for this outsized love. Just the knowledge that I can create love out of nothing, out of thin air. *Bone of my bones, flesh of my flesh!* I am not paralyzed by choice; I will break this body in its pursuit.

When we were young, I thought Jack was a safe space from which I could reach out and touch wonder. Unlike my emotional father, he felt like solid ground, a continent rather than an island. I did not yet know the ways that desire would one day erode his shores. Nor, I suspect, did he.

*   *   *   *   *

My father is alive. My father is not alive. What happens when our most basic assumptions change in an instant? As I weaved my way through my grandmother's rooms on the day of his death, my mother's pills clinking in my jeans pocket, nothing was true. Not the clock on the mantel, ticking off time, or her wool sweater draped over my shoulders. Easier to deny death than to face its finality. If he was dead, then it was also just as likely that he was not dead. I was born back into uncertainty, a transcendent not-knowing; a chasm of love.

"Stalk the gaps," Dillard advises, but here especially I am brought to my knees with love. No wonder my father died young. He was forty-four years old. There is not a helmet hard enough for a life so full of love. But where he succumbed, I grew determined to thrive. In my thirties now, I covet my decade of love and keep my distance from whatever threatens to steal it away—heart-break, tedium, the limits of my human mediocrity. I will not sit down inside the wreckages of love, like a bad girl in a pile of ruined shoes. I want to create something useful with it before it disappears, a hammer, say, with which I might build a ship large enough to hold it, a brush to lacquer its tender hull.

A girl-child, who will better learn to balance the burdens of love.

Or a book of impossible questions.

[EAT IT]

There were signs of what was to come. We should have taken note.

The morning of the flood we are afloat in bed, sweat-slicked beneath the blankets, and though we don't know it yet, the surrounding streets are under three feet of sea water.

This morning, like every morning, I startle to find a full-grown man in my bed. Seven years together and that beard, those wide freckled shoulders. Who the hell *are* you? The air conditioner hums inside the window frame. The man in my bed sleeps. The hollow thud of déjà vus: *Wake up, Stranger.* You moan a tune and roll away. On your nightstand is a glass tipped over during the night, water puddled around spare change, dimes magnified to the size of quarters. Your arms are flung back above your head— your right index finger piercing the puddle like a blessing.

Norwalk, Connecticut. 2011. The early years. You like my laugh still, and tell me so, my face damp in your hands. We stay like this for a while in the gray morning light. I kiss your *kepi* and you whisper the Yiddish word back to me—*kepi, kepi, kepi*—your forehead warm and salty. We have curtains, just like grownups, and they billow in the breeze. It's so quiet I can hear the ocean slapping the sides of the boats at the oyster farm a block away. Just the thought makes me hungry. Only yesterday, we'd untan-

gled our crab traps, packed a cooler of raw chicken, and ambled
down to the docks near our apartment. The day was bright, dry,
and calm, the sky a portentous, porcelain blue. "You could crack
that sky with a spoon," you said. Everything in this town is precious and private, and in all the adjacent towns, too—Greenwich,
Westport, Darien—wealthy seaside communities where you
can't reach the ocean without trespassing. And so we trespassed,
tired of the signs that told us not to, bored by these wealthy people in plaid shirts, their desultory yachts bobbing and empty
against the pier. We tiptoed onto private docks three blocks
from our apartment. A regal white condo building loomed behind us looking bored. It was Saturday and we wanted to catch
crabs and eat them. You can't stand the way they try to crawl out
of the boiling pot, though, so I have to do that part alone, shriek-
ing in terror and delight while you cower in the bedroom, their
blue claws curling out of the water like past sins. "Do you remember when I waited on Jay-Z and Beyoncé at Le Cirque?" I said. It
was the year after we'd graduated from college. I'd recently quit
Teach for America and had somehow faked my way into a job
in one of New York's most prestigious restaurants. You plopped
down on the cooler and looked up at me. "You were a food runner, and they made you leave the food at the door to their private
dining room so the more senior food runner could bring it to the
table," you said. "Yeah, but I smelled her perfume," I reminded
you, "and cleared their plates after they'd gone." You handed
me a paring knife and I kneeled on the dock and gorged a hole
through one wet, pink breast. You splayed the nets out and readied the hooks. Entrails littered the planks, slips of spine, sprays
of flaked and effulgent fish scales, all that dead meat. I remembered a story my grandmother Cynthia told me once, how when
she was pregnant with my father she had these unconquerable
cravings for raw meat. Sometimes, on the way home from the
grocery store, she would unwrap the package of ground beef on
the passenger seat of the car. Every so often, she'd reach over and
pinch hunks of the soft, greasy red meat in her fingers and slip
them into her mouth. She liked the way the fat slicked her lips,

and she'd rub them together for a while afterward, tasting the salt. After she gave birth the cravings disappeared, and ever after she couldn't stand the sight of ground beef. Once, when I was a teenager, I ordered a hamburger at a restaurant and she made me sit outside on a bench to eat it. I didn't see her often then, but after I went to college she took a sudden interest in me, and sent me to study abroad in places like Italy and England, financed trips and clothes and a graduate education I could never have afforded otherwise. She paid for that trip to Colorado, you remember, when you had an interview for a PhD program. She liked the idea of you having a PhD. So did I. It was the poshest thing I could imagine then, dating a doctor. I thought it would legitimize me. What can I say? She had a way of making me feel terribly insecure, like an orphan. My father, her son, was dead, and my mother was incidental, ineffectual, plebeian, Jewish. She would have to save me from her. But when we got to Colorado you decided you didn't want a PhD after all, so instead we spent the week eating takeout on the motel bed and fucking on the floor. After she died, she bequeathed all of her money to her one remaining son, my estranged uncle, thus abruptly ending my dalliances with earthly pleasures beyond my means. I sometimes wonder if it would have been less painful had I not had those experiences, had never known the decadence of flying first class or the perfection of a velvety foie gras from a Paris bistro. Maybe I wouldn't now be so bitterly eyeballing the seaside condos behind us, or tossing flecks of raw chicken all over their private docks like a bratty toddler.

What I never told you: that after Beyoncé left the restaurant in a plume of Givenchy, I ate the leftover meat off of her plate. It was divine.

*   *   *   *   *

Today, the morning of the flood, I pull the sheet over my head and lay on your chest, idly making shapes with your limp penis. A hamburger, a pretzel, a ship with a sail. Do you remember, years ago, I'd gone with Mom, Mommom, and Jessie to see the performance show *Puppetry of the Penis? This exists, lest we forget!* Two naked Australian guys with remarkably pliant cocks telling bawdy jokes and making origami-like shapes out of their genitalia. (And Cynthia thought us plebeian!) By some stroke of luck Jessie was called on stage as a volunteer. By "stroke of luck," of course, I mean that I pointed and yelled until they picked her. She'd recently been hired at Mom's real estate office, after a brief post-college stint as a radio station promoter, and this was her congratulations. The lanky one did a handstand, his balls bouncing jauntily below her chin. I can't remember the point of the trick, only Jessie's astonished expression and Mommom's tears from laughing so hard. This woman who'd refused her whole life to French kiss, a fact my mother never tired of teasing her about. Walking back from the stage, Jessie's face was red and wet from embarrassment. *Fuck you*, she whispered to me as she made her way to her seat. *I love you*, I'd whispered back. *I love you, I love you, I love you.*

What is the difference between the love I feel for my best friend and the love I feel for you? A precise emotion should have a more precise expression, don't you think? Jessie and I have been best friends since the age of seven. What do we have to show for it? A title as fickle as a fourteen-year-old's diary entries? No ring. No legal attachments. No shared air fryer or Nutribullet.

Your cock is fine, I suppose. It passes time. My head is on your thigh and I'm smushing the head of your penis into my eyeball. Why? I have no idea. I don't want to get up. Yesterday's crabbing adventure exhausted me. I disappointed you again, though I like the way your jaw goes slack while you slowly blink at the sky. It's a reaction, at least. Sometimes, I don't know whether I want you to father my children or me. Intellectually they are very different, but emotionally kindred. These are 100 percent bona fide, class A, primo daddy issues. As cliché as the holiday-colored rubber bands Jessie and I used to wear on our braces. Do you sense these competing desires ever, when you're admonishing me for breaking yet another glass? Forgetting to change the oil in my car? Locking my keys inside the apartment so that we have to walk three miles in the cold to the gas station where the landlord works to fetch a spare? I've killed every plant we've ever owned. Scratched your new paintings with the fabric of my winter coat. Gotten my fishing line caught in trees and under rocks so often you won't retrieve them for me anymore. You just cut my line.

And still you love me. Let me use your body as my playground. Nuzzle my nose into your armpits, butt crack, underneath your balls. I scratch your back just to watch your skin change colors. Taste your hair and toes and snot. "You are a monkey," you tell me, "an orangutan." You cannot pronounce this word. I love your smells, the sweat and funk and cum of you. But I also want you to pet my hair and tell me I'm a good girl. To save me from bullies and burning buildings and never, ever leave me. "You are the only person who laughs at my jokes," you say, tucking my hair behind my ear. Which is true. No one else laughs. They are not good jokes.

I get out of bed reluctantly, make us French toast. We sit on folding chairs in front of the sliding glass doors watching the rain. Every so often, I put my foot on the glass and finger the bruise on my knee from where, yesterday, the man had kicked me to the gravel. "You tripped over your shoelaces," you say, "and fell on the grass." I dump more syrup on my plate, then hold the bottle out in offering. You're so literal. "It's tiresome," I say. We can't decide whether to go back to bed or take a walk in the summer rain, such is our life these broke days, beholden only to our bodies' whims and the cantankerous landlord who lives upstairs. Also it's Sunday; Monday morning and our lame-ass jobs are still eons in the future. And all this wet is right here, right now.

"Let's go," you say, taking a last bite before standing up. You wipe syrup from your lips with the back of your hand in the same way that once, years ago, you smudged the too-red lipstick from my mouth. We don't yet know that the town is flooded, the banks well past breached, fishes swimming frantically past the Lane Bryant on Wall Street. You come out of the bedroom wearing your good jeans, a zippered hoody, and the floppy knit hat you don like a uniform from September through May. This is before you start combing your hair to the side and maintaining a perfect five o'clock shadow. Before you begin taking more photos of yourself than of me. Before my laugh starts to drive you nuts. Before the rest of this day, this year, all the years to come.

The phone rings and my heart seizes. He's dead, I'm sure of it. My brother, Eric, bipolar boy-child, addicted to heroin and perennially perched on the edge of nonexistence. But it's just my mother calling to tell me that she heard there was flooding in Norwalk and shouldn't I come home? "How can I come home if the town is flooded?" I ask her. And anyway, we don't see any flooding. She'll do anything to get me home. It will be many more years before we realize the toll this anticipatory grief has taken on our bodies, my mother's and mine. After fifteen years of active addiction, Eric has rendered her maternalism primitive, at times barbaric. When he is well, which isn't often, she is wild, almost manic, with joy. And when he inevitably relapses, often disappearing for days or weeks into the shattered streets of Kensington, Philadelphia, that notorious heroin hole, she erupts in despair and panic. "Well, I have codependence," she snaps. "What do you expect?" As if it were a virus. She drives through the tent cities of Kensington screaming his name. When I left home for college at eighteen, I went as far away as possible and never moved back. I was soldered to my brother like a bell to an anchor. Staying would have meant drowning.

You were my buoy. I knew it and I grabbed on tight.

* * * * *

It seems obvious now that I fell in love with your quiet first. Such stark relief from the frat boys who paraded drunk down dorm hallways, shouting and banging, desperate to be noticed. In contrast, you were slight and handsome, though not nearly as unsure of yourself as you let on, when we were the only two people in the study lounge with our stacks of index cards and handfuls of highlighters. I learned you slowly, eventually, after months of flirting and silent but implied rejection, which only stoked my infatuation. This nerdy, serious boy from Maine. My mother always told me to marry a nerd. "They make money and never cheat," she said.

"I thought you were a virgin," I confessed years later. "You wore those high-water jeans. Had that awful haircut."

There was the one night during our sophomore year, I tried to go down on you in your dorm room while we watched a rerun of *The Cosby Show*. We hadn't even kissed yet. I managed to slide down your pants and place your limp penis into my mouth before you lifted my chin and shook your head slightly, eyebrows knitted.

"That's okay," you may have said.
Or, "You're okay."

I wish I could go back in time, if not to take your penis out of my mouth, at least to recall just which phrasing you'd used. The distinction feels important now, as if it might offer some indication of where we were headed all along. For years, you needed only mention the words "Cosby Show" for my face to flame in embarrassment, which still thrills you. My desire for you then was incomprehensible to me, except as a vessel for my grotesque love. There was the night I pretended to be drunker than I was, just to feel you hold me up during the walk home. "Let me sleep here," I'd whined. Some childish bid for attention. As if I was going to lie down right there in the snow, midway between town and campus, and go to sleep. "I can't do that," you said, clasping me warmly around the waist, my insides pulsing with want. I was near tears in frustration. I didn't talk to you for three months after that; my unrequited love was too painful. It was all so dramatic, like an episode of *My So-Called Life*. In other words, just how I liked it.

It takes patience to love a woman like that.

* * * * *

Behind us on the dock yesterday, gulls circled and screamed hungrily. We sang a song about a turkey wearing glasses, something we made up so long ago we can't remember when. We dangled our feet off the dock and gently dropped the crab nets holding the raw chicken into the water until we felt them hit bottom. It's been a long few months. You hate your new job. You hate every job you've ever had. I think you might just hate working, which I suppose I can understand. I do not hate my job, teaching creative writing part-time at a local college, though it is becoming increasingly clear that this burgeoning part of my identity, the part that writes and teaches and talks about writing and teaching, is not charming to you. For one, I make no money. Occasionally, I drag you to readings in the city and you could not be more blatantly bored. You pick up and abandon pursuits wantonly: guitar, photography, woodworking, painting. You are talented at all of them and satisfied by none. I would like to please you but I don't know how. One problem is that we do not know the future. There is no plan. You might never figure out what brings you joy. My brother could die tomorrow. We will or will not get married, make money, have children, buy houses, have sex with other human beings *ever again until the day we die amen*. I'm developing an insidious suspicion that people can't save one another after all.

This is disappointing. My whole life has been built on this premise.

Cynthia was half-dead by the time I found out about the cancer. She'd told no one. This was a couple years ago. You and I had just graduated from separate master's programs and moved here to Norwalk. I drove like a maniac to her hospital bed in Philadelphia, wild with fear. For three days, she lingered. I was the only one there. Eric would have come, except we both knew she wouldn't want him there. Cynthia didn't give a shit about my brother, and this pained us both. His cardinal sin was being born a boy. She'd had four sons and a husband and resented each of them in turn. If she'd had a girl she would have named her Annie. She could be cruel and cold, Cynthia, although it's equally true that she taught me about beauty. When I was a kid, I rarely saw her except for yearly trips into the city to the opera. Wherever we went, someone was getting stabbed beatifically and she'd squeal in delight. "Oh, Jessica," she'd say, "isn't it *wonderful?*" And it was. All that ornate despair. The opera externalized everything I felt inside, gave it flesh and sound. As I got older, she encouraged my suspicion that art was a worthy pursuit, if not a financially viable one. She assumed I'd find a wealthy husband as she had, though she hoped I'd avoid the requisite gaggle of children all but required in her day.

There were a few months, when I was a kid, when she took me to her housekeeper Icy's Baptist church. Icy was a large Jamaican woman who I loved with my whole heart. She held me under her arm during the sermon, but when the singing began both women leaped to their feet, tossed their gleaming faces skyward, and sang. They *sang.* Together, their distinct vibratos—Cynthia's high soprano and Icy's resonant alto—were like corresponding teeth on a zipper. They cinched my spine and I bolted upright in the pew. I could not breathe. My vision blurred. The congregation swayed, clapped, and cried. The old man beside me beat time on the pew with the palm of his hand. A girl about my size painted the air with her hands. Love was everywhere and everything. How had I not noticed before? Cynthia pulled me to my feet. My whole body filled with sound and I felt myself lifting, as if the music were helium. I grabbed on to Icy's wrist, afraid I might dissolve into Jesus's love, or go willingly, a castaway inside his billowing white robes.

Later I would have a secularist's language for this experience. Art as the pursuit of cognitive ecstasy, a return to something long forgotten. Stendhal syndrome. The earth and its sacred math. But in the moment, I had only this: the sky and its wise, punishing gods.

Icy worked for my grandparents for almost two decades. Cynthia helped her get citizenship, buy her first home, bring her children to the States, only to fire her unceremoniously one day, when both women were in their late sixties, after falsely accusing her of stealing jewelry.

Icy taught me to love loudly, but it was Cynthia who taught me about Stendhal, the early nineteenth-century writer after whom the term "Stendhal syndrome" was coined: overwhelming, visceral reactions to phenomena of great beauty, art, nature, love, any evidence of profound personal meaning. A temple in ruins, say, or a child's bloodied lip. Mother Theresa's profile on a piece of burned toast. A Plath poem. The distant cry of a beluga off the Aleutian coast. Reports consistently mention rapid heartbeat, fainting, even hallucinations. Some people lose their breath, consciousness, or common sense. Loved ones are called and hospital visits are common. There are follow-ups with the shrink. Prescriptions for Xanax. She'd explained it to me excitedly in the car on the way back from Icy's church while I lay spent and shivering in the back seat. I was eight years old and God already had me fighting for my life. Icy drove slowly, occasionally looking back at me and smiling.

"Oh, that's just the Lord, chile," she said smiling through the purple veil of her church hat. "You gon' be irie, baby. You got God in your bones now." I wished my grandmother was driving and Icy was in the back with me, stroking my cheek and telling me about God.

It wouldn't be until years later, picking up Stendhal's work for the first time in college, that I learned that Stendhal first experienced the phenomena during a visit to Giotto's frescoes in the Basilica of Santa Croce in Florence. The young art aficionado had been overcome by the beauty he had previously only glimpsed in books, but also the terror that such beauty implied. According to Stendhal, "God's only excuse is that he does not exist." He wrote, "As I emerged from the porch of Santa Croce, I was seized with a fierce palpitation of the heart; the wellspring of life was dried up within me, and I walked in constant fear of falling to the ground." Stendhal suspected that there are consequences for sneaking a peek up creation's billowing skirt. For fingering the tenuous threads of metaphor.

But not to worry, doctors advise, it's psychosomatic. It's all in your head.

Be wary of your worship, is how I understand it. This is the dark side of wonder. Your art and your gods will bring you to your knees.

By the time I reached her bedside, Cynthia was deep into a morphine coma. Her tongue was dry and swollen and hung limply in the back of her throat. All I could do was read to her from the *People* magazine I found in the hospital lobby, pausing occasionally to paint her cracked lips with water.

At her funeral, Icy wept so loudly she shook.

* * * * *

But, anyway, those glances against joy? I feel them all the time. Like yesterday on the dock, your hand on my knee, the sun on my forehead. That was joy, no? Yesterday, ten years ago, five years hence. Love and fear pressing against the swell of us. I pulled the trap up slowly, hand over hand on the rope. Empty, save for the ravaged chicken breast, already starting to cook in the sun.

The sailboat was well past the first set of buoys before the man spotted us, his head poking up behind the wheel like a jack-in-the-box. "Hey," he yelled. "These docks are private!" We stared at him, our heads cocked to the side like dogs. You tossed the old chicken into the ocean and pulled out a fresh breast from the cooler. The man in the boat was displeased. "Did you hear me?" he called. You waved and smiled, like maybe you thought he was remarking on the fine weather, though of course we'd heard him. It was only when he turned the boat around and began heading back to shore that I started to get nervous.

"Let's go," I said, pulling my feet from the water.
"Nah," you said.

Confrontation terrifies me; testosterone is mystifying. You grinned at him as he approached. He was red-faced and puffy and wore a pink polo shirt that strained at the buttons. He was easily twice your size. I thought about chucking a chicken breast at him, but I'd already planned to make a parmesan with whatever was left over and I really didn't want to go to the grocery store. I looked to you for direction, but you were self-immolating right there on the dock. The sun shifted on its axis and all that was good and benevolent in this world rolled into the sea and sank. I jumped to my feet. I don't know if I was more afraid of the man now raging obscenities as he approached the dock or your implacability while you burned. I felt inexplicably caught between two instincts: fear of him and fear of you.

"Let's go!" I said, grabbing up our stuff. I pulled on your arm. The man pulled the boat alongside the dock, grabbed some sort of heavy black object, I knew not what, and stumble-jumped out of his boat. He chased us for four blocks. At some point, we started laughing and couldn't stop. Nothing was funny and everything was funny. We reached a small pond in front of a neighbor's yard and you flung yourself into the water, giddy and flailing. I fell or was kicked to the ground. The man whipped out his camera and started taking my picture like the paparazzi, one after the other.

Years and years later, after all the grief has passed between us, I'll tell Jessie about this day over the phone. I'll be splayed out on the bathroom floor, days after you've moved out, looking for the button I'd remembered you'd lost on your shirt a few weeks prior. Finding it will suddenly feel imperative. "He told us he was going to hang our mugshots in the lobby of the condo building," I'll tell Jessie. I'll tell her that if I really think about it, I lived off of the scraps of those early days of our relationship for a long time. How you pulled me to my feet, dripping pond water, and stood between me and the man with the camera. That I felt a surge of love nearly take me down again. The man stuttered. You held me. Then, you took his camera and threw it into the pond.

I'll tell her this, too. That the day you proposed, nearly five years later, you led me to the shores of Lake Champlain in Vermont, and all around us the sky and fields and mountains and sun and clouds and even the patient, humming moon looked on and you entered the lake and knelt, your body submerged in the body of the earth, and held up your hands in offer. It was not so much a proposal of marriage as it was a request to keep close and tender for all the days and nights through which we would hurtle through space, in this form or others, mere parts of a sacred whole.

"That had to mean something, right?" I'll ask Jessie, fetal-prone on the floor. "That had to mean something more than this."

"It does," she'll say. "It means get off the floor and go eat a fucking sandwich."

* * * * *

But before all this—before the lake and the ring and the fucking inedible peanut butter sandwich, I'm thinking about love. I'm thinking about love as we wade through the flooded streets of Norwalk, past the shuttered businesses and their frantic owners fruitlessly stacking bags of sand against windows. As the water travels up my thighs and you pull me up on the sidewalk. As little waves slap against shop doors and a girl in a pink hoodie smiles from a third-floor window, her mother behind her and gazing at the sky, her arms wrapped around the child's waist. The storm had been grossly under-predicted. Nobody had been prepared. We'd slept through the whole thing. We'd eaten French toast while all around us the world spilled.

As we walk, we pass detritus from nearby stores: a gold earring, a pound of coffee, thirteen sodden greeting cards, a toy train, a pair of forks. These are the days between our past and our future. It seems we have a decision to make, but we don't know the answer and we don't know the question. We are twenty-six years old, and though we don't suspect it yet, half of our time as a couple has already passed us by. To the west is the known world, the familiar, a highway, a smattering of towns, Starbucks, your beloved Subway tuna hoagies, a Gold's gym. East is the vast ocean, dark and unknowable. We are in the wet center of it and you are holding my hand and pulling me past the jewelry shop I like, the one with little white elephants painted on the windows. Tomorrow, I'll be too sick to go to work. The fever will peak at 104 and you'll briefly consider taking me to the hospital. I'll refuse to go, too hot and tired to move, so instead you'll tuck me into the couch and put on a documentary about assisted suicide that takes me by surprise and makes me weep uncontrollably. You'll feel bad about it, and laugh and hold me until I calm down. "Love," you'll say. "Love, love. Love, it's okay," rocking me back and forth.

Love, like God, is essentially a language problem. "The syntactical nature of reality, the real secret of magic, is that the world is made of words," says ethnobotanist and mystic Terence McKenna. "And if you know the words that the world is made of, you can make of it whatever you wish." I keep thinking that if I find the right combination of words, I might find the key to my brother's sobriety; or your devotion; or this unceasing desire to prove myself worthy of it all. That a secret door might swing open and rain mercy on our weary heads.

Here is a necklace, not the one that had belonged to Cynthia that I'd lost at the beach months ago, but this one made of colorful rings of candy. You scoop it into your hands as it floats past us, pull me close, slip it over my head and around my neck. You look at me and smile goofily. The colors begin to bleed into the skin over my collar bone. A streetlamp flickers off as the clouds begin to drift. People murmur obscenities as they slosh down the sidewalk, kicking debris into gutters. We are drenched and smiling and young and sad and utterly clueless. The candy is nearly dissolved, swirls of pink and green and blue running down my chest. I laugh. You laugh. You put your hand on my chest and swirl the colors together, then slip your finger under the necklace and hold it to my mouth. I would like to pause the reel here, to remember how it felt to love you for one more minute. Then you do. You stand very still for me while the whole world rushes by, and you say something that sounds like an incantation. You say it very slowly. "Go on, Love," is what you say. "Go on, Love, eat it."

[EVERY OTHER WOMAN IS MY TRUE NORTH]

SEPTEMBER 2013

WINOOSKI, VERMONT

I am waiting in a corner coffee shop for a woman with wings. I'd glimpsed the wings on her Facebook profile picture, splayed flat, ribbed, and gray across her back like a bird run headlong into a windowpane. But it's not the wings I admire so much as the laundry line, which is inked up and across her arm and over her clavicle, billowing across the dark crease where her arm ends and her torso begins. The laundry line is draped in polka dot underwear and flouncy dresses, so intricate that I can make out the whorls of wood grain on the old-fashioned clothespins. I scroll through her photos while I wait, imagining us sprawled out on her orange sofa knitting scarves side-by-side. In this fantasy, I am the kind of woman who knits. I am also the kind of woman who drinks whiskey neat, plays the banjo, and looks impossibly cool in Doc Martens. I grow herbs and ride horses and my spiritual practice is polyamory.

I'm twenty-nine years old. Jack and I have recently moved to Vermont after a couple of years in Connecticut postgraduate school. We have a pretty apartment in a town called Winooski, just outside of Burlington, and I teach creative writing part-time at three different colleges. My current sense of self is determined by two facts:

1. My first book, a memoir about my father, will be published in a few months;
2. I nurture a crippling sense of apocalyptic doom most of the time.

I'm desperate for female friendship, a longing Jack understands but only in theory. How do I explain that while he is an island of safety, women are my whole world? I miss Jessie, my first and best friend, and the other close friends I've made in the places we'd lived in our twenties: New Hampshire, New York, North Carolina, New York again, Connecticut. Most of these friendships persist, but the physical space between us stokes an ancient longing.

I have no idea how adult women meet and form relationships, so I start clumsily asking women out on friend dates, women from work, or the gym, or the writer's group I've recently joined. They are just like date-dates, I realize, or how I imagine date-dates might be, given that Jack and I shacked up at eighteen and only went on one "proper" date prior to that, during which I'd ordered scallop crudo in an attempt to seem sophisticated and then balked when the waiter asked if I knew "crudo" meant raw— "Um, yeah, of course"—and spent the rest of the night hungry and holding back tears of embarrassment. *Adult women can court one another,* I realize during one of these dates, even if just for friendship! This realization thrills me. Our evenings are full of the usual seductions and red flags. A colleague named Shama holds the door open to the restaurant and puts her hands on my thighs when we talk at the bar. Gabby lets me pay for our drinks all night and keeps accepting olives from the guy next to her, who is swiping them from the bar and dropping them into her empty rocks glass, which she then stabs with a toothpick and pops into her mouth. Rebecca is humorless, but chic in black leather pants. Dee is a poet and we talk about our students wistfully over steaming bowls of pho. Harlow and I trade sob stories about dead parents while dangling our feet into the cold waters of Lake Champlain, a joint pinched between her fingers. It's thrilling to date these women, knowing I'm not breaking the bonds of my partnership. Friendship between adult women, this new and wild frontier, feels suddenly subversive—cultivated through intention, rather than the inadvertence through which most of my youthful friendships had developed. My intentions and theirs, and the frisson of our womanhood together. While men remain largely inexplicable and off-limits to me, women fill the gulfs of desire where my relationship with Jack ends and the rest of me begins. Of course, my friendships with women are not without risk, but they contain a kind of feminine gravity that soothes me. I have not known a woman to disappear or desert me, to behave with inexplicable violence, or to let her emotions overwhelm her to the point of self-annihilation. These are men's behaviors.

I am yet to realize that my mother's relationship with my brother is just that, a complete breakdown of selfhood. The cleaving didn't finish its work; she does not know where her body ends and his begins. But for now, I still see it as ferocious mother-love, which I do not envy but still admire.

* * * * *

One night, a few months after our move here, I bring home a woman from the local bar after one of many sad, solo ventures out into the world in an attempt to quell my loneliness. Instead of trying to appear sexy and available in a short skirt and pumps, I went to the bar wearing my coolest Neko Case T-shirt and tried to look friendly and interesting. Unsurprisingly, Jack had refused to go with me, not a fan of bars, live music, Neko Case, or other humans, generally speaking. At the bar I watch a local band play and during a break in the show go to the bathroom.

While I pee, I hear a knock from the next stall over, commencing that most sacred of ceremonies between women strangers. "Can you pass me some toilet paper?" the voice entreats. After a few drinks and some decent conversation, I invite her over for a nightcap and to meet Jack, giddy with the flush of fledgling connection. Our apartment is a block away from the bar and it's only ten o'clock, and after all we are young and hungry and our T-shirts are so cool. But as soon as we walk in, I realize I've miscalculated. Under the bright lights of the kitchen, Jack looks annoyed and tired. My new friend's demeanor shifts perceptibly in his company. She takes quick sips of the wine I've poured her and leans stiffly against the counter, skittish as a doe and eyeing us suspiciously. Jack tries to make small talk while I slice a half-eaten wheel of brie and arrange a neat cluster of Cheez-Its on our one clean plate. Sweat blooms on my forehead and palms, my overzealous desire for connection like some unseemly spillage over which I have no control. She glances between us, me grinning awkwardly and Jack yawning, clearly ready for bed. I would cry except the cliché of it might kill me. "Did you think I would fuck you guys?" she finally asks, placing her empty wine glass in the sink.

Now, months later, I've shakily repaired my confidence. And besides, I have an ostensibly good and professional reason for having asked the woman with wings to meet me here in this coffee shop. I reached out because I love her ink drawings—have a few framed and hanging in the bathroom—and I am hoping she will draw the animals for the literary anthology slash Vermont field guide that I'm editing with some writer friends. The project will marry our state's bio- and creative diversity, I'd explained in an email. We'll introduce a species, list its essential characteristics, typical of any field guide, but then also include a short piece of creative writing composed by a Vermont writer and inspired by the species. The final element of the book, our book proposal claims, will be drawings of each species by a celebrated Vermont artist. Would she be that artist? I'd asked.

Before contacting her, I'd scoured her Facebook and Instagram profiles, admiring the wry expressions of barn owls and black-throated blue warblers, winking moose, and round-hipped honeybees. I marveled at her drawings and the tattoos of her drawings on the freckled chests and forearms of her friends. I wondered what it would be like to have her score those creatures into my skin, if I could bear such beauty. In the background of her pictures hang long stalks of drying lavender and sage. Mugs of tea steam on side tables made from orange crates. In selfies, the sun slicks her purple lips and her smile parts as if to taste it.

When she finally arrives, I cannot reconcile the vibrant artist from the screen with the silent, stoic fortress in front of me. The coffee shop hums. We sit down across from another. *Hello. Hi. Glad you could make it.* Her slant-eyed appraisals wring my heart out. Inside the hole of her gaze, I feel both seen and swallowed, which is disconcerting but not exactly unpleasant. She stares steely from inside herself, her dark brown bob like a drawn curtain across her shoulders. I picture myself tiny, scaling her body like the walls of a castle, peering through a window and finding myself there, cross-legged on the cement floor of her heart, centimeters high, waving and grinning like a schmuck. I keep reminding myself that internet people and real-life people are not the same people. This distinction should be obvious, but as Jack says often, I'm smart but I have no common sense. I gave up constructing my internet avatar years ago when I could not figure out which story to tell about myself or how best to tell it. I still don't know what sort of woman to be, let alone which sort of woman I should pretend to be on the internet. I worry that this signals a failure of imagination. If I cannot imagine the woman I should like to be, then how will I ever become her?

The woman with wings orders decaf, welcome cause to dislike her, and wonders aloud why I have asked her here, why we couldn't just proceed with the project over email. I pick up my mug, then put it down, then pick it up. The coffee shop is white and bright as a blank document, the baristas tabbing up and down the long counter. They turn knobs and empty grinds into compost bins, their pretty faces deleted behind clouds of steam. In my nervousness I chatter on about the dynamism of the project, stuttering and repeating myself; the truth is that the few instructions could have easily been typed into an email. So why *did* I ask her here? At other tables, people chat amicably and easily. A toddler in overalls and curly hair runs a wooden block over her mother's shoe then up her calf. The room is warm and sultry compared to the knifing cold outside. I am not yet accustomed to seeing people from the internet materialize in front of me, as if conjured by magic. The canyon of space between us is a wonder; I've made her appear and yet I am powerless to reach her. We watch the child, the woman with wings and I, and laugh nervously into our coffee mugs until she suddenly stands up to leave. Silently, I chastise myself for my over-eagerness, my too-obvious banalities about whimsy and word counts. My dumb haircut. She pulls a red wool bolero over her shoulders and glances around the coffee shop as if looking for someone more interesting to bid farewell. From her canvas tote bag, which is splattered with thick daubs of oil paint, she pulls out her keys and a tin of Smith's Rosebud Salve, which she opens and pats on to her lips. Her boots, I notice, are thick-soled and shiny as pennies. On her right thumb she wears a silver ring, thin as a whisper, that catches the light when she moves. Her hips are slender, spread, and solid. I have a sudden urge to grab them like a steering wheel. Or, more accurately, I want to be grabbed, ridden, rideable, but also a woman who rides. I suspect she is a woman who rides. A woman who both knows and goes after what she wants, who never questions her own identity, who is not plagued by some ancient pain she can't quite name or locate. When I try to ride Jack, my skinny lover, I can't find the rhythm and his penis always slips out. Further evidence of my feminine ineptitude, I figure. Proof of my gaping holes. As I try to think of something to say to keep her here, I stand and my chair clatters to the ground. The toddler beside us screams out in surprise and the woman with wings turns her benevolent gaze toward her, then kneels, picks up the child's wooden block, and holds it in her open palm.

* * * * *

A year later, a woman named Cal joins our writers' group. She is also new to Vermont and we soon discover a shared and voracious curiosity. I recognize in her what I recognize in myself: an insatiable appetite for wonder. I have had plenty of women friends, but never have I landed so deeply in the heart of another woman nor let another woman land so deeply in mine—the first cleaving had been so hard.

Even more than the damp New England forests, she feels a lot like coming home. The ancient Greeks believed women to be wet, cool, and fertile landscapes in need of taming, lest they spill all over themselves. We are like that. We are women who spill, leaking across town and state lines looking for a place to plant our bodies. We've both moved more times than the number of years we've stayed put. We are loudly proud and quietly ashamed of the ways we spill. By that I mean we are hungry for love of all kinds, but we know this is not acceptable. It makes us pathetic, needy, soft. We are confused by the many, conflicting ways we are told to be. We are too loud, too quiet, too smart, too dumb, too chaste, too slutty. We think we are capacious and creative. We desire love, but we also dole it out unreservedly.

"The problem with stereotypes," says writer Chimamanda Adichie, "is not that they are untrue. It is that they are incomplete." I show Adichie's TED Talk, "The Danger of a Single Story," to my students every semester and every semester someone cries. Cal has a finely honed internet self and I admire her canny, her disguise, even if it also confuses me. In real life, she has light hair, plump lips, and a wide, white chest smooth as snow. I imagine laying my head on her chest, as a child might, but don't dare.

From the haze of onebody, I'd learned that women are never one story, only many stories that together make a universe. One story says that women are soft, malleable, and penetrable. This is our oldest story. It tells that women are the embodiment of man's greatest fear: susceptibility to death. Which of course we are.

Susceptible to death, that is.

When I confess to Cal one day, "I scare myself driving alone on the highway, knowing I could so effortlessly flatten the gas pedal, take a hard turn off a bridge, into a wall..." she nods, *yes*, understands exactly what I mean—not a death wish, exactly, but how the power to choose can make you tremble, nearly slip. I've never been good at choosing anything, especially how to be a woman. I don't want to choose one narrative, especially one shaped by the dramatic arc, Aristotle's infamous pyramid, which starts in conflict and desire, rises sharply to climax, and then sputters to its unconsummated end, so uncannily mirroring the male orgasm. That's not a structure that fits my life. Even my orgasms are rounder, more reverberant than that, and anyway so too is womanhood.

Perhaps it's because I don't have a penis that dramatic arcs don't fit my experiences, but mostly I suspect it's because there has never been a time in my life when the death of a loved one was not imminent. As the daughter of an alcoholic father who was always just evading death until he didn't, and the sister of a heroin addict who for the last fifteen years has been hell-bent on running straight toward it, I've never known a time when death's serpent tongue wasn't hot on my tail. In this way, this life of anticipatory grief is shaped more like a circle than an arc. Carl Jung says that "life is a luminous pause between two great mysteries, which themselves are one." Death, then, is a short-cut back to the first great mystery, the "garden of union and innocence," onebody, oneness, call it what you will. The ultimate wonder. A thing for which language is inadequate.

Not *end* but *and*.

Maybe this longing to return is the energy from which artists source their best works, if they can only survive it. Cal agrees. She says she feels it too—the blazing seduction of the slim fissure between life and death—and this makes me love her even more.

We sit in a bar on Church Street after our writer's group one night in February. We love these meetings except for the egomaniacal leader, who is by day a dull, know-it-all public radio host. We toast with glasses of whiskey that we chase with soft, herby deviled eggs that the bartender makes himself. Now that we've found one another, Cal and I do not want to be apart. We make schoolgirl vows and keep them for a while—to be as powerful, prolific, and devoted as Gloria Steinem and Marlo Thomas; Gertrude Stein and Alice B. Toklas; Emily Dickinson and her sister-in-law, Susan, to whom she wrote all those sumptuous love letters. To be "whachers" like Emily Brontë, who employed this deliberate misspelling again and again to mean a kind of spiritual vigilance, which she kept all her life beside the icy, heart-clenched moors. We've been together nearly every day for the last year, Cal and me. We lust after the same art, the same people who are not our partners, and harbor the same longings for reckless adventures. We desire consummation, but with what? (Ourselves? One another? The universe?) Latin: *consummatus*: perfected, complete. To me, that means returning to the beginning. Instead, we make plans to go to Texas and Mexico: hot, dry, masculine places where we can get into trouble.

At night in her living room we write stories and read them aloud to one another while her husband is away on business trips and candles burn into puddles on the coffee table. Her kids' sharp Legos blanket the floor like land mines, and we tell stories for hours about who we have been and who we are becoming. Sometimes, we write the same stories together, passing pieces of stories back and forth, building them as we go, until they grow large and ridiculous and we love them as a mother loves her ugly children. We are trying to rewrite the tropes of womanhood, the ones that say we can be a wife or a friend but not both. That we can be a virgin or a whore, but not both. That we can make children or art, but not both. Or, even more terrifying, the ones that tell us we can make children *and* art *and* money *and* love *and* delicious buttercream cupcakes for the Girl Scouts *and* a perfectly straight cat-eye at five thirty in the morning that won't smudge by five thirty in the evening when it is of course time to make dinner—but we can't do all of those things and not fail at them too. And we can't not hate ourselves for failing. And we can't not hate one another for pretending otherwise.

I watch the way Cal's children desire her, toss their tiny arms around her neck, press their faces into her chest when they cry. The connection is so basic, so symbiotic, so obvious. How had I never noticed before? For the first time, perhaps, I want a baby keenly and not just abstractly. The longing feels almost against my will. When Jack and I have sex, I press myself hard against his body. I want to fill his whole body with my body, to feel his blood and muscles and skin surround me like wet, warm earth. And then I want to take that wet, wormy, writhing earth and mold it into the shape of a girl, to feel her come alive under my hands. I am twenty-nine years old and so full of love and longing and wonder and grief and fear and nothing I make yet satisfies these overwhelming feelings. I cannot write them into submission. A child, a human being, is the only viable solution, the only container vast enough for this energy.

These are selfish thoughts. I'm not even sure I like children in particular or just the idea of them generally. It's distracting, to be subject to such animal urges. I don't want to be subject to my body. I want my body to be subject to my mind. Cal has two kids, and so perhaps my desire to be close to her is also a desire to

draw from that same well of immortality. Of course, it is dangerous. Love is always dangerous. Some nights we drink too much
wine and desperately mash our mouths and bodies together until we fall asleep. One night, one of her children wanders into the
room, sleep-addled, and we lurch apart. Because Cal and I value
recklessness in ourselves, we value it in one another, and exalt
one another. We gaze lovingly into the mirror. In one another
we can love the best of ourselves without excoriating the things
we hate about ourselves. This is a cheaper, temporary version of
onebody, like mistaking a weekend at Esalen for a lifelong mind-
fulness practice.

When I confess to Jack later, he just shrugs. "Women are different," he says. "I don't care if you sleep with women." I don't think,
What of me do you keep for yourself? I am too relieved. Finally, permission to be both. To be and.

It's like discovering a new species, women, perhaps because it's
only now that I feel I am becoming one. In youth, femininity was
the air I breathed, omnipresent and therefore invisible. The shift
reminds me of how Annie Dillard describes learning how to see
in her memoir *Pilgrim at Tinker Creek*: "I'd look ahead and see, not
the row of hemlocks across the road, but the air in front of it. My
eyes would focus along that column of air, picking out flying insects." Women are the strange and luminous insects populat-
ing the air. Everywhere I go are women to admire, creatures wild
and resplendent.

I love the women at my gym. I love the woman whose body is
bathed in freckles and whose red hair is a ripe apple knotted on
top of her head. I love the woman in her eighties, thin as a spear
and Viking-strong, who sways to the music and smiles at herself
in the mirror and whoops when we're working hard. I love the
very fat woman who wears a knit cap and a poncho and dances
with the other women during salsa classes. I love the woman
melting inside her black clothes who wears too much eyeliner

and groans loudly and often. I love the woman in dreads who smells like tomatoes and the woman who always wears a Mickey Mouse T-shirt. There are a few women with whom I sometimes think I'd like to be friends, women with intricate tattoos and flames of blue in their hair, but then I remember that my love for them is a silent, private apprenticeship. I am learning how to be a woman by *whaching* women.

Anyway, what would I say?
Hello, nice squats?

It is a small community gym, a YMCA, and the women I love go to exercise classes. Sometimes I think I only go to exercise classes to see the women. I like moving my body in tandem with other women's bodies. It feels like prayer. It feels like balance. It keeps me sane through the deep winter in Vermont. It is almost always deep winter in Vermont. We are old and young and thin and fat and we take all sorts of classes. Some of the classes require us to lift dumbbells many times in a row and most classes involve music so loud that the voices in our heads are temporarily, mercifully drowned out. There are classes with big inflated rubber balls over which we drape our bodies and classes in which we try to dance sexily, mimicking the instructor's body with our own bodies. There are classes during which we ride a stationary bicycle like a whip-cracked horse and classes that teach us to hold imaginary thumbtacks inside our belly buttons. There are yoga classes that make me feel as if we are onebody, breathing in and out together, and holding very still together, and clenching our vaginal muscles together, and thinking *mula bandha* at the same time, and often this makes me feel good, like activating the collective unconscious. Like pressing the ON button. My favorite part of the yoga class is the end, when we play dead together, and sometimes one of us snores softly or passes gas and we are just women in bodies on a wooden floor.

———

I do not know what I believe in if not women in bodies on a wooden floor.

As it turns out, Emily Brontë never made a friend in her life, Charlotte said, and died on the sofa at two on a winter afternoon. She was thirty-one years old.

But maybe *love* is not the right word. I am still not sure how to differentiate between overwhelming feelings of admiration and good will, and the specific love of a person. Surely my love for my mother, say, or Jack, must be separate sentiments than my love for these women or even Cal. It is sloppy to glob these emotions together, except that I have no other name for how I feel. For their unabashed expression of their bodies, the women at the gym are perfect to me. We are losing the fight against mortality together. Together, we beat our bodies against the tide of entropy.

To speak, I fear, would be to shatter this exquisite illusion.

"Divine perfection is the ability to recognize, forgive, and include imperfection," writes Richard Rohr, whose newsletters pop up in my inbox daily. Maybe *love* is simply my secularist's way of saying *God*. Shorthand for *whole*. Easier to forgive imperfections at a distance, whereas I am unable to forgive myself, and my mother, for ours. Yesterday, she called me on her way home from an appointment. I was polishing off a bag of potato chips at the time. She was at the drive-through at McDonald's. "Mom! That shit will kill you," I'd yelled, and hung up the phone.

* * * * *

I love women in a way that is occasionally erotic, but always visceral. I suspect this has something to do with archetypes—women in myths and stories across cultures and time—the narratives that form the framework within which we conduct our little lives. Stories instruct us about the complexities of life. Stories enable us to understand the need for and the ways to raise a submerged archetype. Who has not lusted after the Femme Fatale? Or draped herself in the soft, cotton cloaks of the Earth Mother? Or donned a ponytail and nonprescription black-rimmed glasses and fancied herself Nancy*motherfuckin*Drew? (Or—*for shame!*—sweet, soft-lipped Snow White, in need of rescuing?) Who has not hunted down a woman with wings from the internet, mistaking her beauty for benevolence? Her vision for kinship? Just me?

My mother was a wild child until she wasn't. Then, for a brief time, we were onebody. Soon after, she became a Single Mother. Then a Suffering Mother. This is the archetype she's clung to the hardest. Mary Magdalene but without the piety. Jung considered the Mother the most important archetype because she contains so much. There's a reason she shows up frequently, a symbol of earth, country, nature, church. Intellectually, my mother understood that her role in my brother's life as his Suffering Mother, his enabling caretaker, did not sustain him. In certain moments she could also admit that her behaviors only hastened his death. And yet this exaggeration of the suffering, sacrificing mother role was a story she couldn't shake. Archetypes are innate projections, part of the collective unconscious, Jung believed. They are not made by us, but *of* us. Observed, but not invented. She didn't choose the Mother archetype; she *was* the Mother archetype. Stories, like bodies, are born and grow and wither and die and dissipate into the earth and grow again—into a tree, say, which then bears fruit that is plucked and eaten and is sometimes poisonous and sometimes not.

After that first meeting with the woman with wings, we communicated only via email. I told myself that I'd just wanted to make a new friend, but deep down I knew the truth. I was hoping she would teach me something about how to be a woman and an artist. I'd thought I could glean some of her confidence, like a hum-mingbird drawing from a flower, and learn how to fulfill my oversized creative lust without getting pregnant. But women are always being asked to share what little power they possess in this world. And why should she? We are all daughters torn from Demeter's fertile field.

* * * * *

Speaking of stories, I prefer to go to the movies alone. Every time I leave the theater, I am either twirling or stomping, gazing wistfully at streetlights, or charging headlong into traffic, em-ulating that film's particular heroine. I want to *be* that woman, whoever she is. After watching *Who's Afraid of Virginia Woolf?* seven times one winter, I wore pencil skirts and red lipstick for a month, drank bourbon, and smoked unapologetically. Later, after the movie's spell wears off, I feel embarrassed. Why can't I be, by myself, a real woman? Real women are not archetypes, I know; we only slip archetypes over our heads like stocking caps. Real women are not characters in a story. Real women tear at the seams of story, trying to regain the sense of wholeness we knew as girls, before we knew better. Before we were wrested from the bellies of our imaginations and told to be pleasant.

In any given moment, the type of woman I am depends on the company I'm keeping, and my crazy ideas about who they want me to be. Will I ever grow out of the need to be *liked*? I wonder. For a time, once, I became the sort of woman who drank green juices made of spinach and celery and took probiotics. I'd been in Los Angeles nannying for a model and her rich and beauti-ful husband. The beautiful husband explained to me that af-ter he got sober, he decided to surround himself with other beautiful people. What's so wrong with that, he wondered, and didn't I think I should lose a little weight? For my birthday that year, they bought me a colonic, and so for a time I also be-came the sort of woman who weeps while a sturdy, elderly Russian woman inserts a tube into her ass and wipes sweat from her brow. I was taking hole-filling literally then. The first time I kissed Cal was a few days after watching *Blue Is the Warmest Color*, a French film about beautiful lesbians. I thought maybe I could be a beautiful lesbian, too, and that would make me interesting in the way that the beautiful lesbians in the film are interesting. Maybe I could be beautiful, and lose a little weight, and be interesting. I never learned how to move beyond the compass of other women. Every other woman is my true north.

The beautiful lesbians in the film smoked cigarettes, and so I bummed a cigarette after I left the theater, but when I glanced at my reflection in the windows of the passing storefronts, I saw that it did not make me beautiful after all, only ghostly. I saw myself evaporating inside the cloud of smoke, just as I'd watched my mother with her cigarettes for decades, conjuring her own disappearance.

*   *   *   *   *

And so it became that Cal and I also condoned and excused one another's bad behavior, finding virtue in what became a wild pursuit of something, I can't remember what. I remember we refused to feel shame for wanting so much. We dreamed up a business: a local writing center. We wanted to create a space for writers in our community to come together. We'd offer writing classes, readings, editing services, rent space in a hip downtown office, and get asymmetrical haircuts. It would be *so cool*. "We'll become big fish in a little pond," she said, and for years I'll wonder if that was a sign I'd missed. It was deep winter in Vermont. The frozen mountains around Burlington were cradling and ominous, and Lake Champlain was paralyzed with ice. We sat in the bar. We sat on her couch. We paced and then sat on the curb and watched our breath unfurl in the gray. One day, we sat in a café and she called her parents who agreed to lend us ten thousand dollars.

We tried to build a business of services for artists, but we balked and called it a collective. The unseemly ego, we knew intuitively, had to remain tucked out of sight. We worked hard all the time and privately we were very high and mighty about it, all that working. We wanted art *and* money and we would not be made to feel bad about it. People showed up. Writers, readers, wannabe writers and readers. Our list of services was longer than our list of clients, though. We couldn't figure out the right balance.

Jack and I were fighting a lot back then—all that working, he said, and still no money—and sometimes I stayed with her for days at a time. One day, I became convinced that he was having an affair with a colleague and so he kicked me out for a time. I was paranoid and jealous. The affair, after all, "was only emotional." There was truth to my jealousy, though. It was only a fluke that I'd guessed right this time. There'd been dozens of others about which I'd been wrong. The fear of losing him was real and overwhelming. It didn't take a therapist for me to figure out why, but it would take a damn good one to help me through it.

When I went out of town to give readings of my first book, Cal had to bear the burden of the business alone. I also couldn't quit teaching until the business was solvent, and though she didn't have to work another job, she did most of the parenting of her two boys while her husband was away. Meanwhile, on the other side of town, a man gave away all our spoils for free. While we charged for writing workshops and editing services and panels comprised of literary agents and local editors, the radio host offered them gratis. He was building a money-less empire. *Art is not commerce*, he wrote to us in an email. He'd turned that original writing group, the one we'd abandoned more than a year ago, into a business just like ours and our two factions were fighting over scraps. In the white blank of the coffee shop, he looked at us and wept.

"This is my legacy," he said. "I can't have children; my girlfriend is forty-five already. This writing center is all I will ever have." I'd felt sorry for him then, and maybe even loved him a little, because aren't we are all just trying to get back home?

What is right? we wondered. We had reached too high, demanded too much. There was not enough business to go around. We felt wretched. "I just want to be a big fish in a little pond," I remembered Cal saying, but even then, I knew she was lying. I wasn't sure I wanted to be a fish at all, and maybe she resented my ambivalent ambitions. Were we building a business for writers or for our own fragile egos?

Only now we wondered alone. We didn't want to show our doubt. Rather than distrust our own intentions, we split and distrusted each other. We still recognized ourselves in one another, but we began to see only that which we disliked most. I think we both thought the other was too self-interested. Too hungry. And we *were* hungry. We hungered for validation. We hungered for experience. We hungered for love. Our business adviser had warned us early on: "Ninety-nine percent of business partnerships end in a splintering of the relationship." But we hadn't believed her. *Not us*, we thought. Then one day one of us called the kettle black, and so it was, and so we were. It was time to (c)leave. We packed up our fliers and business cards, the desks we had built so hopefully. We had to go back to being ourselves alone. There it was, the consummation we had so desired, an end to a friendship.

Sometimes, I think I am haunted by women past, present, and future. I am learning to hold them in my body like wonder, like a wound that doesn't hurt but is still an opening. The other day, I read a memoir by photographer Sally Mann. After a fleeing convict killed himself in the woods on her Virginia farmland one day in 2001, she decided to drive to various Civil War battlefields and take photographs. She wanted to know if the earth remembered the carnage it had witnessed and subsumed. One evening, she walked onto the battlefields near the Battle of Spotsylvania Court House with her dog Honey, who promptly began digging into the soil to make himself a bed. "The smell of that soil came up to me; the smell of ancient bloodshed, of bodies plowed under, all part of the land, part of the earth I was breathing, the creamy smell of the feminine force in the world. That force is Death, dark, damp, implacable creator of life, the terrible mother who nourishes us and by whom we are, in time, consumed." It startled me to see her calling death a woman, and then it made perfect sense. All those damp, dark Greek stereotypes came back to me. All the women who haunt me, even here in the pages of this book. The bodies from which we came are feminine; so too the body to which we will return.

Now I content myself with women who are not twin spirits, but safer because of it. They are old friends, mostly, and some new, and of course the women at the gym, whom I love passionately and from a distance, where they remain perfect to me. I understand that even a child would leave me (we would cleave), and I would leave her (die), but it is lovely to imagine that life—like the best stories—moves in a circle, is always beginning.

[SMOKE]

"Did you steal my lighter?" she asks for the fifth time. I am smoking with my mother on the back patio, visiting her in Philadelphia for a week during the holidays, the slate steaming in an unseasonable heat. The dogs have been dead for years, but I hear them panting beside us in the dark and reach my hand out to stroke their warm phantom necks. Bailey, the red retriever, was so anxious he rarely left my mother's side, preferring his big head nuzzled between her legs like a horse in blinders, or a nun her winged cornette.

My mother has been smoking for forty-three years. If you were to collect all of my mother's cigarette butts they would fill a dumpster. My mother cannot make it through a meal without a cigarette break. Her house and clothes and skin and hair and car and blankets and even her three fat, irreverent cats are soured in smoke. My mother is fifty-eight years old and smoking is the great solace of her life. Instead of lovers, she holds cigarettes. Cigarettes are her constant companion because life is sad, she says, and then, offering evidence, "My dogs are dead."

When I visit, I insist she smoke outside and she grunts and calls me a hypocrite, which is true. I chastise her between long pulls on the cigarettes I buy in anticipation of these visits. I love smoking with my mother. I can't figure out why; can't square that circle. It would not be enough to simply sit outside with her on the patio for ten minutes at a time, complaining about this and that and talking about what's wrong with everyone we know, which we're very good at doing. Our talk is more interesting with a prop, a rhythm, a contained time frame demanding we get to the point. It's the fire around which we settle to tell our stories. She is happiest with a lit cigarette and I am happiest when she is happy. That red circle of light in the dark is as familiar to me as fear itself. It is both a harbinger of doom and a Pavlovian guard against it. We sit on fraying wicker furniture and watch a deer-shadow stalk across the yard, backlit by the shopping center lights.

Christmas night, 2013, seventy-five degrees, and my mother has been limping. Military jets from the nearby base pass overhead and the ground shudders. A week ago, she tripped on the patio steps in the backyard of her friend's house, smashing her knee and face into the stone. She had been smoking outside alone when she fell. Inside was a small party. She stumbled into the mudroom and sat on a wooden bench. "I heard voices in the living room," she says, "and I tried to call out, but no one heard me." The room dimmed and she lost consciousness. When she came to a few minutes later, she vomited on the floor. A doctor ran some tests the next morning, wrote her a prescription for Percocet, and sent her home. "You may have a concussion," the doctor told her, "but then again, maybe not."

"I fell asleep when I got back and when I woke up, I was not in my body. I don't know where I was. I was elsewhere," she says. Later, when I'm in bed and she's smoking and coughing downstairs, I'll think about what she'd said about being outside of her body and start to panic. Sometimes I fear she will cough herself right out of her skin. How can I remain embodied when the body from which I grew and cleaved is no longer a body, is *elsewhere*? The urge to return then, to go back to the beginning, is unbearable. I feel as desperate as the dead, red dog, wanting to push my way back inside of her. The doctor recommended two weeks in a dark room. No television. No reading. She lives alone and will not obey the doctor. "Well, what the hell would you do in a dark room for two weeks without TV or books?" she asks. I consider her question seriously. What *would* I do? "Masturbate," I say, nodding solemnly. I am trying to distract her from *elsewhere* by making her laugh. It's not working. She nods, takes a final drag, and stubs out her cigarette. She doesn't think I'm funny. "You're really not that funny," she says. Between the three of us—my mother, my brother, and me—I am the least funny, which they remind me often. "*We* are funny," they say. "*You* are only *kinda* funny."

"Anyway, when's Jack knocking you up?" she says, pocketing the lighter in her sweater. The casualness of this question is feigned. I know, because she asks me all the time. I reply just as casually, as if I could take it or leave it, but we both know we're having a different conversation than the words connote. Sometimes I wonder if getting pregnant is the only way to return to onebody before dying. Sometimes I wonder if her insistence on my having a child convinces me this is true. It is only an accident of etymology that "cleave" has two opposing meanings: to come together and to break apart. Like twins separated at birth, or Jung's "two great mysteries, which themselves are one." I picture these mysteries of existence curling back into themselves into a lush and ecstatic whole. I also get the sense that my having a child is the only way she will feel sated with her life's work, and it's a lot to bear. Historically, men are charged with carrying forward the family legacy, but also, historically, not the source of that labor.

*   *   *   *   *

There were three others with whom my mother had once shared her abundant body. Each one cleaved prematurely and against her will. She didn't choose to tell me about the abortions either. Cynthia told me one night when I was thirteen and sleeping over at her house. I was shocked. I thought I knew everything about my mother. The hubris of youth!

"So, who made you get the abortions?" I asked her the next day.

Her mother.
My father.
His mother.

"Everybody," she said. "Everybody was against me." By the fourth pregnancy, she was twenty-four years old and she willed me alive. And so we also share our onebody with three ghost bodies and of course the boy-body, who every day threatens to ghost. The poet Wang Ping offers this word: *teng ai*. "A love embedded in preverbal knowledge, accompanied by unspeakable pain, and shared only through the empathy between the two bodies (mother and daughter) alike." Once, my mother said to me: "Most of the time, I think you are mine alone. I forget that there was another person involved. I think I created you all by myself." Virgin Mary with a pack of Marlboro Lights.

Years later, she'll offer me a framed photo of my father, decades dead, steering one of the old, rented Island Packets he used to sail around the Chesapeake Bay. It is my favorite photo of him, face turned to the sun, his blond hair mussed in the wind, the white sail behind him catching the salted air. "I can't," I'll say, handing it back to her. "It makes me too sad."

"Oh, god," she'll scoff. "He's been dead for so long." But what she means, I know, is that she does not believe he deserves my grief, and maybe she resents me for feeling it, as if grieving my father in some way diminishes her dogged, earthly, maternal work.

* * * * *

After we finish our cigarettes, my mother and I make prime rib for dinner. It is a quiet, melancholic Christmas. Eric calls from rehab threatening suicide again, but it is a ploy to get us to take him from the rehab in the country to the psych ward in the city, where he can leave voluntarily and go score. He didn't take the cleaving well either, this boy-child, and thrashed around until he found a new way to fill his holes: heroin. "You know what I'll do if you don't come," he says. "You *know*."

He is mostly dead already, I think. His death is the imminence through which my mother and I move through our days. When he is in jail, we say, *Hooray, he's in jail!* What we mean is, *temporarily safe from himself.* Other things we cannot, will not, say aloud.

"No, no, no," she tells Eric, "I won't take you."

But she will, and we both know it, and so does he. After dinner, to console ourselves, we decide to make a fire in the fireplace. My mother sits on the sofa, nursing a glass of wine. The dogs have been replaced by cats, three of them, who orbit around her legs and occasionally slap one another across the face. "Newspaper?" I ask, after I've bucketed the ashes and readied the fireplace.

"I'm out," she says. "Use my bills. There's a basketful in the kitchen."

Later, upstairs in bed in the guest room, I hear the television click on and her lighter spark. I listen to her cough. I set up a fan. *Shut up*, I yell silently. *Shut up.* I can't stand her cough. We're in the middle of a heat wave, the warmest Christmas on record in Philadelphia. Outside in the dark, my mother's gladiolas break soil, shudder, then sway. ("The apocalypse," we'd whispered over cigarettes, the steam rising from the slate, the backlit deer in the corner, her hair blue and blown in the blaze of a passing jet. We have no idea of the apocalypse to come, only a few years in our future.) That night, I lie in bed and consider telling Cal that

I don't want to build the business with her after all; that I want to get pregnant instead. I don't think about telling Jack this plan, which I'll only realize much later. In the morning, my mother posts pictures of our prime rib dinner on Facebook, her littlest cat in the bathroom wastebasket.

How many likes did I get? she asks every half hour.
How many now?

Social media, too, offers the illusion of wholeness, and anyway, it's cheaper than children and cleaner than death. Immortality in the twenty-first century.

*   *   *   *   *

Back in Vermont a week later, I'm still thinking about my mom's question about getting pregnant. I wake up and think *I can't have a kid because I do not want to make mommy-friends.* I'm making this list up as I go. It's distracting and boring, this child-lust. Wouldn't it be more fun to jump on a plane to San Miguel tomorrow? Or buy a laundromat in Mexico City and watch tele-novelas all day? Or spend a year in Amarillo practicing stoicism and the two-step? Take my mother to Siena, Italy, and set her up with an easel, oil paints, and an ashtray?

Instead, I dream I bury my rib in the backyard and grow twins. They float behind me all day like balloons, squawking in the back of my classroom while we discuss narrative arc and unlik-able characters. (Is there anything worse than being *unlikable?*) I assign a writing prompt—two pages about whatever—and lock myself in the bathroom. I thought that having a child would mean expanding the body we had shared before we cleaved, and to do so would keep this onebody from ever dying. To keep *her* from dying. *Why do you believe getting pregnant will save your moth-er's life?* I ask the mirror. The little black balloons bounce up and down behind the stall door, appearing and disappearing, then expanding and shrinking, taunting me. Lungs, I realize. Her lungs are haunting me like angry children.

When I get home, Jack has made ribs for dinner, and I try to remember that coincidence is not the same thing as meaning. I laugh like a maniac. "What?" he asks, bewildered. "You're laughing like a maniac." I don't tell him about my dream, but that night we have sex on the kitchen floor. I don't poke a hole in the condom like my mother suggested, but I consider it.

*   *   *   *   *

A little over a decade ago, when Jack and I were in college, a girl with cherry-red hair and a tattoo of Buddha on her wrist came barreling into his dorm room in the middle of the night. She was a friend of a friend—he knew her only peripherally—so when she barged in screaming, all he could do was stare.

"This is me!" she'd shouted in the doorway, her face twisted in rage. "This is me!" He remembers a line of snot running over her lips. He remembers her hair moving in all directions like Medusa. What could he say? *What is you? What is me?* I didn't know her well, this flame-haired woman, and I kept my distance. I sensed that whatever was bright, feral, and enraged in her was also in me, and if I got too close, I might erupt. Form is flexible, this body, but not immutable. I didn't move all the way to New Hampshire just to lose my shit now. This was before social media. These days, people do this sort of thing all the time, publicly perform pain, only now we are less conspicuous about it. Behind our screens, we craft our calls of distress as pithy tweets, overadjusted selfies, or photoshopped pictures of our breakfast cereal. *This is me*, we cry out. *This is me.* When I watch my mother smoke and cough, she is also in part performing her pain. Playing a role. Caught in it.

Sunday, the morning after kitchen-floor sex, and I'm editing student essays while Jack is on his computer browsing Facebook. He sees that the girl with the cherry-red hair and a Buddha tattoo is dead. People are posting on her wall, letting her know that they are sorry she is dead and wish for her a peaceful afterlife, which strikes me as polite but possibly misdirected.

Miss you, they write.
Love you.
RIP.

Meanwhile, on the bottom right corner of his screen, a green light next to her name indicates that she's online. *Thank you*, she replies to the well-wishers. *I love you, too.* How can someone be alive on the internet but dead in life? Jack opens a private message box, and then hesitates. *Hello?* he writes. He sits back on the sofa, his hands still poised over the keyboard. For a long time, there is nothing. Then, something.

Hello, it reads.

How are you? he asks. *Do you remember me?*

Remind me, she says.

And he does. His name, their interactions, the occasional lunches during which she always ate peanut butter and jelly sandwiches, which he'd found charming and tells her so.

He waits several minutes, watching three blue dots indicating that she's typing, then stopping, then typing again. Then nothing for long while. He waits, and then she finally replies.

Erin is no longer with us.

He waits and watches the screen.

This is her mother, it reads, and then the green circle turns red.

One day, the rumor goes, we will upload the contents of our brains onto the internet where we will remain bodyless and immortal. In her grief, I thought, this mother was only trying to hurry the process along. "The condition of motherhood demands that you learn to give birth to someone who won't last," I read recently in an essay by the poet Franny Howe, "to love someone who will leave, to teach a person who will suffer anyway, to put a life before your own . . . to have a job that you can never quit." Here she was, mother of a flame-haired girl who had suffered and left her (so much like my mother's son), not quitting. Not so different from the daughter trying to write her mother into immortality—to hold her in time and space with nothing more than black marks on white paper. Not so different from my mother, rescuing my brother from himself again and again (if only for one more brief stay), and not quitting. Smoking and smoking and not quitting, as if becoming and annihilation are the same.

If we can't become without dying, then we have to stay in our bodies and deal. We have to bear our *wundes.* On the other hand, the artifact is heartier than the flesh-child, Howe says, which the artist can "swing from a noose, bang on the ground, stamp on, throw in the water, and send into battle against the outside world," and reading it I think, yes, better stick with art.

*   *   *   *   *

In the beginning, there is a woman sitting on a couch holding a burning cigarette. Beside her are three fat, irreverent cats. It's Christmas. Upstairs, her grown daughter traces circles in her mind, trying for sleep, fighting the urge to go downstairs and curl into her mother's lap, knowing it wouldn't make life any less sad. Instead, in the dark, in the bed that has never been her bed, she dreams up her own girl-child and holds up her winged body like an offering, like atonement for everything she cannot deliver.

This is me, she whispers. *This is me.*

[ILLUSION OF SAFETY]

Recently, a friend mentioned that there is a group of nuns living here in Vermont: two hours south on the interstate and a half mile up a mountainside. He was visiting me in the cubicle farm where the adjuncts are stuffed. We sat across from one another at my borrowed desk, my friend and me, his eyes dark and bright. For years he'd suffered with drug addiction, but now, at thirty-seven, he's found wonder in Catholicism and carpentry instead. He even looks like Jesus, I teased him. I told him I wanted to visit the nuns. One day I will just jump in my car and go. Perhaps they can show me what will happen with this love, where it came from and what to make with it. There is a giant monastery at the top of the mountain and a garden where they grow food. The nuns make dolls of yarn and dinner from the garden. They sleep in rooms no bigger than a casket. They pray behind bars of iron, ecstatic with love. It seems to me the nuns have found a channel for their love, I say, a safe place to put it, a single name to call in the dark. What is prayer except a means through which we bear our love? I'd find Jesus too if I could.

The nuns are always praying, he told me. He told me they were praying *right now*.

I imagined their prayer as ritualized, rhythmic, abiding. They do not waver in their prayer; they do not pray with abandon.

Their prayer is disciplined, safe. They pray for the living and for our dead. They pray for our very souls.

"They even pray for you," my friend said, putting his hand on mine, and his earnestness was not lost on me, his extraordinary compassion.

"But you are wrong about one thing," he said gently, looking at me squarely now. "Prayer is anything but safe."

[MERCY]

There was a time, years ago, when Jack and I spent a long week-end in the mountains of Vermont, about two hours from home. The cabin was on loan from a friend. It had been sitting vacant for months, so we had to clean it out before we could stay. It was early fall and we were giddy. It is possible we were playing hooky from work. It is possible we were playing out a fantasy, something utopian and wild. It smacked of naivety and Thoreau, our being there, and it is possible we made love outside and contracted poison ivy in inconvenient places. Nevertheless, on the first day I grabbed the kitchen trash can to empty it, screamed, and dropped it on the floor. Inside, a mouse had shredded an entire roll of toilet paper, cardboard included, to make her nest. Beside her were five, tiny newborns, blister-taut and wriggling. I laughed.

"Babies," Jack whispered.

"I was just surprised," I think I said.

Twelve black eyes stared up at us, frozen. I remember thinking it looked cozy in there. I wanted to toss the mice into the woods and retain use of the trash can, but Jack wouldn't have it. "They'll die if we do that."

Slowly, tenderly, he bore the trash can deep into the woods behind the cabin and left it there intact. He moved like a child carrying his grandmother's fancy teapot. I kissed his mouth then, and his breath warmed my face.

In the morning, curious, we crept over in our sweatpants and reckless hair. We clutched our coffee mugs and shivered. We sipped and sipped.

When I tell you she took mercy on her children, I mean their heads were chewed off. I mean most of their organs were gone, eaten, their fur in bloody clumps, the toilet paper damp and black. It means, I'll learn later, that she panicked and chose to save herself. Chose to sacrifice the pups rather than leave them to horrors unknown.

It means she was gone, baby, gone.

When I say it was a gruesome scene, what I mean is that five tiny skulls were shattered, and all the bones picked clean. She was wretched with mercy, is what I mean. What Jack did next, though, that must have been it—the first moment I saw him as a father—watching him bury those battered bodies in the brush. Then watching him walk away.

[THE CREATIVE IMPERATIVE & OTHER INCONVENIENCES]

I leave the Vermont tundra and drive nine hours south to Mom-mom's tiny condo in Margate, New Jersey, to spend the next three weeks trying to unfuck my novel. That this is potentially only a three-week process is one distinct advantage of art over children, I've decided, who usually require years of therapy to get unfucked. Mommom's eighty-five now, sprightly and bossy as hell. She calls upon my arrival from her home in the suburbs of Philly, reminding me again to keep the doors and windows locked, not to turn the heat up past sixty-five, and make sure I turn off the stove after I use it *every* time. ("Like *every* time?" I ask. "*Every* time!" she replies.) The next morning, I wake up early and sit on the patio with my coffee, shivering and listening to the wind whistle down the empty street. I can't yet face the fail-ure of this project. It's all I have to show for the last three years of my life, the only manifestation of my wellness while my brother sells phone cards for junk drugs in Kensington. Across the street, the condo windows are dark. Winter in a shore town is a carni-val up and disappeared. By late September the tourists have re-turned to Philadelphia and its suburbs, leaving behind their broken beach chairs to rust beneath the boardwalk, their empty popcorn tins and pizza boxes and gin bottles and chicken bones and Popsicle sticks and cheap plastic flip-flops overflowing the trash cans—until the old homeless women come around with their metal shopping carts to pick through it all. Trash men charge behind, readying the town for autumn's surge of bluster-ous man-boys in pressed white shirts and gold watches, eager to win a little something on the craps tables, spending ever more in the bars and clubs—toasting to women, the night. By February the few locals remaining are waitresses, realtors, or card dealers. Atlantic City hovers on the horizon ensconced in clouds: a city in trouble. Casinos are blinking out one by one. Trump Plaza is just another giant headstone in a crowded graveyard. From the porch off of my grandmother's condo, one town over in Margate, Atlantic City's silhouette resembles a gap-toothed smile, bright lights interspersed with black. Carapaces where once thousands of people roamed the halls and filled the restaurants, gaming rooms and hotel rooms; laughing, drinking, smoking, fucking.

* * * * *

Once, about seven years ago, I took Jack to Atlantic City, his first time. We were celebrating Jessie's recent promotion at work and accompanied by her usual coterie of admirers. We roamed the gaming rooms, drinks in tow, played a few hands of blackjack, and then retired to a bar. It was not, decidedly, Jack's scene, his scene being his own living room. Earlier, a drunken bartender had chastised him for wearing his tweed golf cap inside the bar and Jack, thinking he was joking, kept his hat on. Moments later, two massive, bald, and glistening bouncers showed up by his side, eager to escort him out. He'd laughed, bemused and a lit-tle startled, and we'd followed them out gladly. *What a world!* But now, at yet another bar, Jack was tiring of the lights, the com-pany (growing less cogent by the minute), and the rattle-tattle of the money machines. He left to walk the boardwalk alone and when I found him, half an hour later, he was shooting baskets at a carnival game and handing out oversized stuffed animals to the small gaggle of kids who had gathered to reap his winnings.

They cheered him on as he sunk one basket after another, the barker leaning lazily against the wall, a cigarette parked between his lips. I remember a dark, solemn girl in glasses and a boy, her brother I guessed, winging balls into the air like missiles. Their mother tried coaxing her kids away and Jack waved her off, smiling—*it's okay, it's fine*—and handed the boy another ball.

Was it that moment, so long ago, watching this man delight in the children's delight, beneath the bellying moon, that I began to formulate the new narrative, the one that had seemed self-evident for so long and has since grown caustic, limned in sadness?

*   *   *   *   *

For the first week of my writing retreat in New Jersey, Jack pleads with me to have Skype sex. I try, but there's no way to turn off the video of yourself, and seeing my own naked body reflected back at me is distracting. I can't relax. Instead, I send him a series of naked photos that take a long time to get right. I put them in black and white to camouflage cellulite and stretch marks and purse my lips slightly but seductively like I've seen other women do. The whole production feels tawdry and ridiculous. He wants me to look severe and dominating, but in this way we are not sexually compatible. I am aroused by sounds, not static images. I need the smells and slickness of skin to get turned on, if not in person, then inside the suppleness of my imagination. Porn is okay, but the pageantry of it annoys me. I like watching the heat rise on someone's cheeks, the sounds of their real and hot breath in my ear, the ache and arch of desire. Not a close-up of a dick pounding into a pussy, or high-pitched squeals as cum drips down someone's chin, or the whips and straps of a woman's gifted power. The pictures I send him are all pretense, too, but I want so much to please him.

I've been in New Jersey for thirteen days when I get the call from my mother. Eric has been missing for the past five days. The purgatorial pall that his heroin addiction has cast over my life for the last ten years is temporarily lifted, if only because I suddenly have something I can do. That's the lie of false agency. In brief moments, I can feign control. In truth, my actions don't influence his. I cannot write him into wellness. Still, you could do worse than to call on me during an emergency. While I spend most of my days in some blind panic or another, the siren's call returns me to myself, to the conditions in which I am most familiar, and therefore most calm. The rhythms of routine baffle me, I am useless in following protocol, but give me disaster and I am like a snapped sheet, starched with renewed utility. This is not to say I am heroic. I can't even save my pennies, let alone thwart whatever threatens life, limb, or sanity. But I will be an implacable wall against which you may bounce ideas, lay your hands, or bash your head. I will take action when action is necessary. I will drive the car through the night to Tulsa, if need be. I will stack the canned foodstuffs in the basement, deliver the test results, tape the windows, call the area hospitals and jails, wash and rewash the linens, listen without offering unsolicited advice, mind the children, notify authorities.

If I am not in my glory, I am at least in the present tense.

The little condo becomes disaster headquarters. The Women descend from their homes outside of Philly—my mother, Mommom, Aunt Carole—and we begin again the usual preparations. Time is now vertical. We can forget work, errands, forward momentum. There will be no new book, no new life. In restriction is a kind of freedom. A singularity of purpose.

My mother calls the usual cast of characters: Eric's spastic girlfriend, Robin; a cop she knows; a spate of friends including the one who works at Friends Hospital in Philadelphia, the dual diagnostic–mental health facility where we plan to rush him should he surface. If you say you're suicidal, they can't turn you away. Everyone knows that.

"We should prepare ourselves for the worst," Carole says, because that's what she always says,

"Where's my purse?" says my grandmother.

I call the emergency rooms, look his name up on various "Inmate Locator" databases, scroll the city's arrest logs, and surreptitiously search the morgue's missing persons site. We send texts to a phone number we are pretty sure no longer works: *Just let us know you're alive. PLEASE!!!*

* * * * *

Once, when we were kids, Eric and I found a squirrel shivering behind the kitchen trash can and something primal and violent rose up in us. We decided to kill it by drowning it in a bucket of water. The scratching was terrible and we plugged our ears with our fingertips. Afterward, Eric wept for three days, but not before scooping the soggy, dead squirrel from the bucket and burying it beneath the forsythia bush. He didn't want our mother to see the monsters we had become. I will never forget the look on his face when he pulled the creature from the bucket, the water dripping as he carried it outside, all that wet shame pooling on the kitchen floor. He was nine years old and bore this duty with stoic acceptance.

I call upon memories from our childhood as if they might offer some clue as to why Eric is an addict and I am not. I want to know what separates us, because if I could find the difference, then maybe I can save him. Rationally, I know better. I've memorized this line from one of my favorite essays, "The Limit," by Christian Wiman, and recite it to myself often: "There are things that happen to us that, no matter how hard we try to forget, no matter with what fortitude we face them, what mix of religion and therapy we swallow, what finished and durable forms of art we turn them into, are going to go on happening inside of us for as long as our brains are alive." Addiction is like that. It doesn't end. It will never end, even if he manages sobriety someday. Even if he dies young.

Anticipatory grief rattles inside of me like a loose gasket. Its very irreconcilability is a point of wonder. On good days, that frisson generates urgency and gratitude. On other days, most days really, I am as skittish as a war veteran. Every darkening cloud is an omen of his demise. A ringing phone sends me into a blind panic. Electrical wires hum overhead, a signal that in this moment, now, he suffers; he is snuffed out.

In this way, addiction leaves us marooned, banished to an ever-present now. My brother's recovery is a ship circling a mile off-shore, ignoring our calls of distress, threatening to dock. Is *this* why I crave a child? To assuage this anticipatory grief? If his imminent death is inextricable from my desire to have a child, it is also why I try so hard to sustain my relationship with Jack, to have a career, to make art—as if I might erect a wall of legacy to save me from the pain of losing him.

Art and children: how else to thwart death?

When he finally surfaces, having run out of energy and stuff to hock, we rush him to yet another hospital. He is pale and sweaty and smells like sour fruit and piss. His hair is falling out in clumps. I drive over the bridge and into the city with both hands on the wheel while our mother sits in the passenger seat holding a lit cigarette to the cracked window. A wet heat rises from the marshes, the smell of brine and decay, while planes descend overhead into Newark airport. I watch him in the rearview mirror. He lays his head back against the seat and mutters, "My runs are getting shorter and shorter," and then closes his eyes.

* * * * *

Afterward, I get back to work at the condo. These rescue missions are not new. I've learned how to keep going, more shakily each time, but forward. I fall into strange hours, waking at noon and working on the novel until late afternoon, when I walk the beach for a couple of hours. I take my lunch at dinnertime: a couple of fried eggs and some blueberries, or a scoop of cottage cheese, a handful of potato chips, and maybe a salad if I have any vegetables. Sometimes, I just eat the tomato whole, not wanting to be bothered by the chopping and dressing. Then, I work until midnight, when I'll eat dinner, some concoction I've thrown into the Crock-Pot earlier in the day. As much as I appreciate good food—and can cook well enough when I have a mind to—I don't enjoy it much alone. The effort feels extraneous, like making up the face that no one will see. Some days I don't eat meals at all, instead grazing on whatever's handy from the fridge or cabinets. Baby carrots, an orange or two, bowl after bowl of Frosted Mini Wheats, stale licorice, or my grandmother's sugar-free ice cream sandwiches. This would not be an advisable diet for a pregnant woman. After so many days alone, I start to devolve. That's the difference between Jack and me. He doesn't come undone. His implosions are silent storms, which is what makes them so scary. He does not talk to me when we drive from Vermont to Maine to visit his parents. Instead, I watch his jaw swell with gritting teeth, staring headlong down the highway for eight lonely hours. When I accidentally drop a window shade on the table he'd recently refinished, the air drains of oxygen. I gasp. His eyes turn razor blue in rage, and a page inside me rips. And yet it's been so long since I've had a conversation with anyone face-to-face that I talk to myself during my daily walks on the beach, exclaiming at what I find washed ashore, like a toddler delighting in her new ability to affix object with sound.

"Tern!" I say, coming across a flock camouflaged by jetty stone. "Rope!"

"Dead crab!"

"Used condom!"

Jack, on the other hand, relishes time alone. He protects it fiercely. After work, he sits quietly on his computer, or when it's summertime, snips at things in his garden: the towering tomato plants, the delicate herbs, the recalcitrant brussels sprout plants that never yield. He digs holes and bangs hammers and makes beautiful working lamps out of nothing more than fishing line, say, and an old busted tuba. Sometimes, I peek around the corner when he's making things and he shoos me away. Sometimes, I refuse to be shooed and put my face on his face and he puts down his tools.

I turn toward Atlantic City, which is three miles down the shore. As I walk, I place treasures in a plastic bag: russet-colored conch shells, driftwood in the shape of a boomerang, a pair of infant Ray-Ban sunglasses in perfect working order. A purple shell older than any narrative I dream up. These objects seem newly charged since I am now one of the few humans around to discover them, and maybe even more so because another time of year would unleash so many more filchers to these shores. The few other souls on the beach are old men. I see one or two a day, sweeping their metal detectors over the sand in slow circles and listening intently. It looks almost religious, this listening. A miracle, I think, to hear what doesn't make a sound.

By the time I reach Atlantic City I am exhausted. I stop in a church parking lot and sit on a cement stoop. The church resembles an old factory, white-bricked and soot-caked. A block of abandoned scaffolding and smashed glass, the smell of burned popcorn and stale beer, pawnshops, broken ATMs, stray sneakers, dive bars open and occupied by nine in the morning, boys selling water bottles and boys selling dope. Boys toss an empty can of peanuts back and forth in the middle of the street and a man in a white Hummer drives between them, appraising the women on the corner.

In the parking lot, a ghostly looking girl in a long nightgown and an overcoat pauses to squat against the side of the building, pees long and hard, then picks up her plastic bag full of T-shirts. The puddle she's left behind steams in the winter air. She toddles over to me and offers a blue T-shirt emblazoned with Trump Plaza for five dollars, smiling, the white lace of her bra, visible behind the unzipped coat, winking in the sun. I buy it for three dollars in quarters and dimes and two menthol cigarettes. It's the first human contact I've had in two weeks, since The Women went back home.

"I took up smoking to get closer to God," she says, tucking a cigarette behind each ear. Sometimes I wonder if I conjure ghost-women or imagine them instead. They are embodiments of my greatest fear, that to let go of fear would be to become them. The scorned, the rejected, the tossed aside. I could easily go mad, I think.

For three days and nights, I am obsessed with a three-minute video on YouTube of twin newborns submerged in a sink of water, umbilical cord still attached, coiled together like lovers, a pair of giant hands holding their heads afloat. I never thought I'd become the kind of woman who spends her days searching YouTube for videos like this one, the kind labeled "cutest ever!" or "Made me cry!" or "AWWW×1000!" They feature puppies and kittens and babies, once a tiny animated shell named Marcel, life in miniature, creatures as batty and oblivious as the person I seem so bent on becoming.

* * * * *

Jessie comes to visit me for the weekend. We met at a swim club where both our grandmothers were members when we were both seven years old and chubby, sporting bangs that bloomed over our foreheads, rogue waves that our mothers would hairspray into place. I spotted her near me in the shallow end of the pool and we stared for a long time in the unabashed way of children—curious about one another but too shy to say hello. She was alone too, jumping on and off a kickboard, and so to impress her I sank to the bottom of the pool, waited a beat, and then pushed off the ground and burst through the surface of the water, whipping my head back so that my hair arced through the sky and then slapped my back, a spray of water droplets glimmering in the sunlight for a long, suspended moment—just like Ariel from my favorite movie, *The Little Mermaid*. This was a signature move for many an American girl born between 1980 and 1986, and it worked. I saw her eyeing me out of my peripheral vision, no doubt hypnotized by the height of my jump, the surface area of my spray, the grace of my arched spine. I grabbed at my inner tube, which was the hottest commodity at the swim club that fateful year, 1991. All the kids fought over them, and if you didn't arrive by 10 a.m., you could forget about getting one unless you made fast friends with a kid who was leaving early. As my admirer approached, I tried out a friend-making tactic I'd been practicing in anticipation of that fall's imminent move to a new school: I fled. But first I had to secure the safe return of my inner tube.

"Hold this while I eat lunch?" I asked, holding out my prized possession.

In Jessie's version of this story, she waited patiently while I scarfed down a grilled cheese sandwich from the snack bar, then sunned myself for the requisite twenty minutes before returning to the water. *We're totally gonna be friends*, she thought while she waited.

"Thanks," I said when I finally returned, taking back my inner tube and swimming away. Later that day, when our grandmothers introduced us—they'd been sitting next to one another observing our ill-fated attempts at friendship and had discovered that we'd both be attending the same elementary school in the fall—she said her name was Jessie. I'd always been called Jess or Jessica, but despite my awkward behavior I was enamored with this other Jessica and thought our shared name might make us best friends forever.

"I'm Jessie too," I said.

And so I was, for at least the first couple of years at that elementary school, until it became too hard for people to distinguish us and a unilateral playground decision was made: I would go back to being Just Jess.

And Just Jess loved Jessie more than she loved anyone in the world.

Just Jess watched her move effortlessly from friend to friend on the playground.

Just Jess felt incomplete when Jessie was not around.

Just Jess was a touch pathetic, but loyal. She would eat worms if Jessie told her to but thank god she didn't.

Instead, Just Jess was a major loner until middle school, when Jessie took pity on her and invited her along to the movies with the cool kids.

And Just Jess was like *Boom! I made it, suckers!* and ditched her two and a half nerdy friends after that.

When we were twelve, Jessie and I smoked pot for the first time out of a bowl made of tinfoil inside her grandmother's garage. Then we panicked and hid behind the silver Continental, chewing gum for four hours.

At thirteen, we skipped down the street on our way, we thought, to lose our virginity. Only she lost her virginity that day. I wouldn't lose mine for another few months—to a boy twice my age who fucked me on his cement basement floor and who I never saw again.

At fourteen, we stayed with her hip aunt in New York City who let us drink margarita mix with the tiniest splash of tequila and then took us to a Sisqó concert where we sang along to the "Thong Song" and whispered excitedly to one another about how drunk we were. The next morning, we were allowed to walk around a neighborhood flea market by ourselves and stole from various vendors fifty-seven plastic butterfly hair clips, some of which had papery wings that fluttered as we moved, and waltzed back into the aunt's apartment wearing them all in our hair at once, looking to all the world like we might lift off of the ground at any moment. "Where'd you get the money for those?" she asked, and we balked, having forgotten to prepare an answer.

At sixteen, Jessie found me passed out on the floor of our friend's boyfriend's condo, having been roofied by the boyfriend and his drug-dealer friend. She frog-marched me past the boys and out to her car and drove me home, but not before dumping a shit-ton of Ajax into their bottle of ketamine. For weeks after that, we feared for her life. The drug-dealer was notoriously violent and the drugs she'd ruined were worth a lot of money. Thankfully, we never saw him again.

By seventeen, we had slept side-by-side in my single bed for so long and so often that it was hard for me to sleep without her there. "Are you guys gay?" my mother asked us one morning, after barging into my room to find us sleeping together again in that tiny bed. She didn't care, her tone implied; she just wanted to know. It had never occurred to Jessie or me that she could have slept in the guest bed.

When my father died, she didn't leave my side for three months.

That same spring, she was stoned on her way to pick me up for our high school graduation and hit an old man crossing the street with her boat of a car. "More like a love tap," she said later. He flailed and fell over, "totally overreacting," and we chalked it up to her infamous bad luck. "Only Jessie," we said.

At nineteen, she visited me at college in New Hampshire and I drove us drunk in that same car to a nightclub in Boston on Halloween. We made it safely, but then I smashed it into a pillar in the parking garage. Shrugging into our glittery angel wings, we went inside anyway, our costumes trailing fairy dust in our wake. Later, when the car broke down in the middle of a bridge on our way back, neither of us was surprised. A trucker pushed us to safety, where we sat on a curb in our tattered costumes at three in the morning watching an old vet pace silently back and forth in a pointed Navy cap while we frantically dialed her mother two states away with the last minutes left on her pay-as-you-go cell phone. She only just managed to get out our location before the phone died, and so it was nothing short of miraculous when, an hour later, a tow truck appeared and took us back to the motel where we were staying. In the morning, we had to walk three miles into the city to Western Union—hungover, broke, and embarrassed—to collect the loan that would cover the car repairs. I don't think we ever repaid her mother. I know I never paid for the damages to her car.

At twenty-three, her dumb boyfriend pissed on the carpet inside a Holiday Inn and she called me crying. "I have the worst luck with men," she wailed. "I'm never dating again." A week after her dumb boyfriend pissed on the carpet inside a Holiday Inn, Jessie met Jon without an H. He was sweet, earnest, and very clumsy. At the restaurant the night of our first meeting, he managed to spill three glasses of water and drop everyone's silverware on the floor in the first fifteen minutes. I loved him immediately, which was even more important to me than the fact that she loved him immediately.

Eight years later, she married him. Before her wedding, we put on our dresses and had our makeup done by a hot chick with an Amy Winehouse–style bouffant and tattoos of animal mash-ups that don't exist in real life. A bear with horns. A dog with wings. The photographer had a funny-sounding French name and followed Jessie around the hotel room like the paparazzi, while her stepmother followed the photographer around the hotel room like the paparazzi, while her younger sisters began to bicker, and her older sister complained about her makeup, and the flower delivery guy inexplicably muscled his way into the hotel room with bouquets and stood waiting for acknowledgment, and before I knew it Jessie was red-faced and panicking and I thrust a giant shot of tequila into her hand and she swallowed it down and felt better and said her vows just fine.

Later, I was a little too drunk to give my toast, sweating in the spotlight in the middle of the ballroom, and I went on for so long that the audience began to clap in the middle of my speech, not cruelly, I thought, but just because they thought I was done.

The joke was on them, though. I wasn't even close to done.

Now, at thirty-two, when I visit Jessie in her new house with her new husband, I crawl into their king-sized bed between them because I still don't understand sleeping under the same roof with Jessie unless it's beside her. "Just let her stay," she mumbles to Jon. "She'll just come back if we kick her out."

Today, she eyes my seashell collection skeptically as she enters my grandmother's condo. I have them aligned along the windowsill in ascending size order. I've washed them meticulously with soap and hot water and applied a thin layer of clear nail polish to their smooth, pale undersides to bring out the gradations of color. They remind me of summer, sunsets, and the fleshy part of my grandmother's arms where the blue veins are like slow-moving rivers.

"You doing okay?" she asks, holding out a handle of vodka in one hand while picking up a shell with the other. She'd recently fielded about twenty calls from me when Eric was missing, and though I've tried to convince her otherwise, she's not sure I'm keeping it together.

"Atlantic surf clam," I explain. "You can tell by the ridging."

"Mmhmm. Cool. Why don't we go out for dinner?" she says. "Did you pack a bra? A different pair of pants? Maybe a pair without a drawstring?"

"I have crackers but no cheese," I say apologetically.

"Get in the shower," she says.

"Maybe a can of tuna, but only the shitty chunk light kind."

"Shower," she says.

"Wait, just let me show you this one video on YouTube!"

When we were teenagers, a few of us often gathered at my mother's house after school since it was close by. My mother was always working, and the refrigerator was usually all but empty. Most of our meals were takeout or frozen, or on good nights we might have some kind of boiled meat smothered in cream of mushroom soup. But Jessie was a magician, Rachael Ray for the latchkey generation, whipping up gourmet meals out of potato chip crumbs and chicken broth.

"Give me the matzo, cream cheese, that half of an onion, and a can of tomato soup," she'd order. I was never hungry until she appeared in the living room thirty minutes later bearing something more delicious-looking than anything I'd ever seen my mother make. For this service alone, she earned my worship.

We go to dinner at an empty bayside steakhouse left over from the eighties. In the center of the circular dining room stands an enormous plastic tree trunk, about twenty feet around, its leafless branches spreading out into thinner and thinner tendrils across the ceiling. We order martinis we don't really want but think we do, then duck into a dive bar for beer after dinner, drink one, and then decide to walk home singing what we can remember of *The Little Mermaid* theme song, down the dark and abandoned streets of this make-believe town. Simultaneously, we are ten and twelve and sixteen and thirty-two. We are the same girl living out different branches of a single tree—Jessie in Pennsylvania where we grew up, a title officer for the real estate company where The Women work, me in Vermont as a writer and pseudo-professor—both of us feigning maturity as best we can. Except for when we are together and become again a single, chubby girl-child with blooming heart and hair and hungry in the same amorphous, desperate way of girls who can never get enough love. We sing: *I've got gadgets and gizmos aplenty. I've got hoozits and whatsits galore. Thingamabobs, I've got twenty! But who cares? No big deal? I want moooooore!*

We never dreamed of weddings, or children, or homes in the suburbs. Why would we have? Nothing about that life seemed happy or interesting. All the grownups we knew were divorced and hated their jobs. We were cared for, but nobody had time to raise us in the traditional sense. My mom was single and trying to keep us alive on her own. Jessie's mother had a boyfriend and a full-time job that occupied most of her time. Her dad had a whole new family. We floated between empty houses, grabbing snacks where we could, pooling our quarters for soft pretzels from the cafeteria. When her sister had a baby at fifteen and moved in with their elderly grandmother, who lived in a condo across the street from our high school, we'd skip school to smoke cigarettes on the porch and change diapers. We knew intimately the futility of that suburban dream; how it never fit girls like us. We fantasized aloud about our future only once, when we were sixteen and stoned and decided we would move to Amsterdam one day, buy a pushcart, and sell prerolled joints and THC-laced baked goods. We'd once had to make pushcarts out of Popsicle sticks for our English class in seventh grade, and so this seemed as viable an option as any other. Not one adult we knew had the life they had planned for, if they'd ever had a plan, so it never occurred to us to *think ahead*. We did whatever came up next—college, boyfriends, jobs, proposals. Sure, okay. The pushcart was a good idea and I stand by it.

And so it was especially funny when we realized last summer, tipsy after the launch of my first book, that we'd somehow come full circle. Soon after starting second grade, the fall after I first met Jessie at the swim club, my mother had convinced me that the best way to make new friends would be to throw a party and invite all of my classmates. I loved books, she'd figured, and so why not make it a book party? Every kid would bring their favorite book and we'd trade via some complicated version of musical chairs.

This party did not, in fact, make me any friends at my new school, and for years Jessie was pissed that she'd had to give up her favorite Nancy Drew hardcover for some kid's old *Peter Pan* paperback. "But here we are," she mused at the book-launch after party, twirling her wine glass. "Twenty-five years later and I'm still going to your fucking book parties."

It is a strangely mild night for February as we sing-walk back from the bar, so we sit on the porch while the streetlights blink yellow and play cards and smoke cigarettes. We both quit smoking for real a while ago, so we decide this doesn't count. Later, we sleep side-by-side in my grandmother's bed and when I wake up the next morning she is gone. I shuffle into the kitchen and make a pot of coffee. A few minutes later, she returns with a bag of bagels and cream cheese and a plastic Rite Aid bag that she leaves on the table while we eat. It isn't until I've finished my breakfast that I notice the pregnancy test inside the plastic bag and jump out of my chair, knocking over a vase of fake sunflowers. I look at her gaping and she's smiling like, *Holy-shit-I'm-nervous-but-also-excited-but-also-like-how-are-you-going-to-react?*

"What the fuck is that?" I say.

"I really think I'm pregnant this time." I knew Jessie and Jon had discussed getting pregnant vaguely, but not in any real way. *We aren't ready!* I want say. *Wait for me!*

"What the fuck is that?" I say, because no other words are forthcoming, and because suddenly my brain has short-circuited and I feel nothing and everything and also an overwhelming fear and love and grief, like I've lost her already. I'm too busy panicking to consider her feelings. She's going to give birth, and fall in love, and abandon me. We are no longer rebellious teenagers, haven't been for a long time. The identity that we forged together so long ago is but a figment of the women we have become. Intellectually, I know this. Emotionally, I am still a little girl who doesn't want to be left behind. A snow squall covers the row of condos across the street like gauze, so that all I see is my row of seashells on the windowsill and the black blur of her Jeep parked out front. I don't want her to leave me here, alone in this desolate town. "What the fuck is that?" I say, pointing at the bag. "What the fuck is that?" I make a silent wish for the snow to keep falling until we are buried, stuck inside this condo forever. Until she gives birth right here on this linoleum kitchen floor.

If she's going to become a mother, then I am too.

* * * * *

On the radio during my drive back to Vermont from New Jersey, I listen to Terry Gross interviewing the astronaut Chris Hadfield about his time in space. At a certain point during his journey, he tells her, he has to leave the ship to fix some doohickey. *Spacewalking*, it's called. Holy shit. He will walk in *space*.

Out he goes.

He wears the suit, the helmet, the gloves. He clings to the tether that keeps him bound to the spaceship.

"I have to interrupt," says Terry. "That's just mind-boggling." Terry's laughing, but it's nervous laughter. I understand. Space *is* terrifying. Its endlessness embodies all our deepest fears—the ones we admit to and the ones we can't even name. The ultimate wonder.

The astronaut agrees.
Earth is over *there* now.
Hello, Earth.

He says, "You are inexplicably in-between what is just a pouring glory of the world roaring by silently next to you, just a kaleidoscope of it. It takes up your whole mind," he tells Terry. "And when you look left, it's the whole bottomless black of the universe. And it goes in all directions."

My mother always chose the pouring glory of the world, even when she wasn't given a choice. In the story of my brother's life, he cried nonstop for the first two years, always too close to the black that preceded him and the black too soon to follow.

How can I make that same choice, knowing how she grieves her son every day?

I do not say to my mother, *but you gave birth to an addict.*

What could she say? It's such a complicated story.

What I hear the astronaut say: *Go placidly amid the noise and haste.*

What if we love gently, patiently, fearlessly, come what may?

I want to say to Jack: *Turn right. See? The pouring glory of the world. Hold my hand.*

I'm no longer sure if love is something we make or something we surrender to. I know, for me, it is as easy as slipping out the door.

"Amen, astronaut," I say to the astronaut. And this prayer, it goes in all directions.

In the novel my protagonist understands what I am yet to: that in the midst of the *pouring glory of the world*, wonder is also in the purple shell, the length of rope, the second of eye contact between one woman and another in an empty parking lot, wherein an obsolete blue T-shirt changes hands. Wonder is accepting what we cannot control, which is damn near everything. This, the pouring glory of the world. It goes in all directions. Wonder is the space between your best friend's baffled expression and her trembling hand, clutching another fucking test we just can't pass, knowing we'll take it again and again. "I was so sure," she whispers, tossing the plastic indicator in the trash. We take a deep breath, Jessie and me. I don't take her hand, though I want to. Instead, we get dressed. We clean up the kitchen. We put on our coats. We step out onto the porch and squint at the snow. She picks at something invisible on her lip. She's wearing a red hat and I see that she is beautiful, a face of pure horizon. I grab a shell, a giant, scalloped blood ark, and head toward her car to clear the windshield.

[CONFESSION]

Jack does not confess of his own volition. After a long night of odd behavior and tedious, Beckett-esque conversations, what he has to say just dawns on me, like a fly materializing from the heat register to land on my lotioned face. He shuffles in and out of the bathroom, looks at me in the mirror, then turns toward the toilet. We got engaged last September, 2014, after dating for eleven years. Why we waited so long was unclear to both of us. We'd been busy, I guess. Marriage, like other such ordeals, seemed an unnecessary distraction on our journey toward whatever-it-was-we-were-supposed-to-be-journeying-toward. As Jack mooned through the apartment, I'd been preparing for bed by applying both an anti-wrinkle cream to the thin, blue skin beneath my eyes and a salicylic acid anti-acne treatment to my forehead and chin, which seemed ironic to me then, fighting both youth and old age on the same face. The face, however, was impervious to these efforts; it stared back defiantly. *Touché, face.* Jack slinked in behind me, grabbed the floss and hovered. The next day, winter break would commence, three weeks I planned to spend on that solitary writing retreat at Mommom's condo to work on the novel I was trying and failing to write. I mention this only to underscore the liminal hour, and Jack's timing, which was ever more inconvenient the longer he dawdled beside the toilet, a string of floss dangling from his incisors like a snapped fishing line.

I studied his reflection in the mirror. His beard is a brilliant burnt orange that contrasts with the feathered bark of his hair, his blue eyes. Gone, the sinewy compactness of his twenties. When we were younger, I avoided being on top when Jack and I had sex because his chest was narrow and taut as a robin's, a delicate cage I might fracture with the weight of my want.

"I'm crushing you," I'd say.
"Crush me," he'd say.

Now, his bigger, softer body absorbs these thrashings, takes and gives back in equal measure. Still, I am too loud. *Shh*, he whispers. *Shh, the neighbors.* "The neighbors" are two twenty-year-old boys who live upstairs. I imagine they don't mind. In fact, I imagine lots of things about these boys, especially since one of them recently dropped his poetry manuscript in our mailbox with a sweet note asking for my feedback. I still feel badly that I never gave him any, too wrapped up with my own students' work, and perhaps a little put off by the title, *Hard on You*. Anyway, I'm tired of being *shh*ed.

Jack is softer now, but broader too—solid as the old lumberjack he recently painted in oils onto a six-by-four-foot canvas, and who now lives above our bed, looking on disapprovingly. Solitary men are his muses. Men with axes and patches in their Carhartts. Men of a certain hour. Men like his father, who worked in the same Maine paper mill for forty years until the day it shut down unceremoniously in 2009, laying off 207 workers—a formidable loss for a town of only 3,187 people. Having grown up just outside of Philadelphia, it took me longer than it should have to comprehend the magnitude of the mill's closure. It took driving through Jack's hometown on an August evening years ago, windows rolled down, passing by the shuttered laundromat and beauty parlor, askew FOR SALE signs on abandoned properties, the windows of the one remaining restaurant, The Chuck Wagon, empty of patrons, and the train tracks next to which an old-timer named Jim used to sit in a metal folding chair every day, rain or shine, wrists crossed over the top of his cane, lifting a hand to passersby. Jack would drive us past him again and again when we were there visiting his parents, just because he knew how much it delighted me to wave back. Jim's death had no direct correlation to the closing of the mill, but I can't help but feel one anyway, some sort of cosmic shift that let slip the old vet from his tenuous perch on this planet.

Jack plucks the floss between his teeth as if tuning a piano. Then he lets it dangle from his mouth while he unbuttons his pants and turns toward the toilet. Suddenly, I understand.

"Oh," I say, my fingers swirled in face cream as he pees behind me, my hair hoisted precariously on top of my head, the single bulb above the bathroom mirror humming. "This is about the kid."

He flushes the toilet and turns to face me, naked, his soft penis bobbing gently, face flush. A single drop of urine drips to the floor. I feel my hair fall and tumble over my shoulders, lisping across my spine. He inhales sharply and pauses. He looks stricken, or I must, because his knees buckle and he reaches for the doorknob to steady himself. I tilt my head to the side, appraising him.

"You don't want the kid, do you?" I say.

"The kid" is what we've come to call our future child—or, I suppose, the future child we'd once planned on making. Neither of us is much interested in two or three, despite the ardent protests that *You can't have just one*. But had we planned it? Or had I simply assumed? That's the trouble I'm having now.

* * * * *

Soon enough, in the novel I am trying and failing to write, the protagonist is trying and failing to convince her husband to have a kid. (There is a bathroom, a fly in the ointment.) I have a vague idea that if I can convince this fictional husband that the kid is a good idea, I will also be able to pull it off in life. The protagonist can't decide if convincing someone to have a child is good juju. What if he resents her after the child is born? What if he really doesn't like the kid they make together and the kid is doomed to suffer the wrath? What if she destroys his life, a life that he "likes," even if liking your life seems to her a reductive argument?

I am trying to remember when I first started to formulate the story of our lives together as parents. Was it early in our relationship, when we took his young nieces to a local zoo and he chased them from exhibit to exhibit while they called to him—*Uncle Ick! Uncle Ick!*—until he ran them down and tossed their tiny bodies into the air while they giggled and screamed?

The reverent burial?
The boardwalk?

Or was it much earlier still, when I was thirteen, long before I met Jack, and babysat regularly for a four-year-old boy named Rory? Rory's father was a "Wall Street guy," though I had no idea what that meant at the time, and his mother wore a shattered expression—which proved, my mother explained patiently, that her husband was screwing other women. I was a kid who liked to know what things *really* meant and learned early on that grownups almost always speak in code. *Off the wagon* meant my father would not be home for some time. *On the wagon* meant breakfast at eight. Saturday could mean Sunday or Monday or never, depending on nothing I could control. Rory and I watched a movie called *Big Rock Candy Mountain* every afternoon from four to five. Then we wrote stories on the sidewalk in chalk, gifts to our adoring public.

"To posterity!" I said.

"To pasta!" Rory said.

Afterward, we liked to draw pictures. I drew the faces of people he knew: Mommy, Daddy, Jessica, Rory. When I finished, he would have me start over, drawing each face again, their names printed neatly below their chins, and *this time no hair*. If I drew his daddy's mustache, he'd get upset and make me erase it. Rory liked to crawl up my shirt, lay his head on my bare stomach, close his eyes, and suck his thumb. Sweet, doe-eyed Rory; he liked this most of all. What to make of a boy so tender, a tuft of hair would send him reeling? His little head on my stomach was an unknowable universe, starred with private wonders.

* * * * *

Shit, I think, as Jack collapses beside me on the bed. We'd talked about this, hadn't we? Did I suspect all along that he didn't want the kid? Has he always known? Is it because he never had a close relationship with his parents? Is it because he does not love me? A length of floss falls from his hand to the floor and I reach for it, shove it back into his hand. "Put it in the fucking trash."

Our wedding is seven months away. In the closet hangs a dress in off-white lace; an empty vessel into which I am to pour my body at the appointed hour. A man named Tucker to minister our vows. A woman called Dandelion to pin my hair. Fifty-two RSVPs requesting lamb shank, twenty-three Cornish game hens, seventeen eggplant napoleons.

I hadn't *known* I wanted a child until recently, since our engagement, when time seemed to speed up. I'd perceived it abstractly, had taken it for granted, *believed* but hadn't felt the urgency. I'm not sure when the desire became imperative, visceral, what trick of biology invaded my body, what surreptitious force. In a philosophy class once, the professor had drawn a distinction between belief and knowledge. "Knowledge must be verifiable," he'd insisted, "which is problematic. Can you see it with your own eyes? Is there an overwhelming consensus among experts?" In my twenties, I'd been unnerved by the conventional way my life seemed to be unspooling. I'd gone to college, met a boy, fallen and stayed in love. We moved around a bit after college, like many white, middle-class twentysomethings. We'd gotten master's degrees and spent a couple of years living apart, driving back and forth between my apartment in New York and his in Connecticut. It was never the life I had imagined for myself, though I couldn't remember what that had been exactly. I knew only that I was my mother's child. Women like us don't love and marry healthy men. We save men from seedy motel rooms and the sides of highways at odd hours of the night. We lack perspective and savings accounts. We love mightily and loudly. Most definitively, though, we become mothers. We mother. But nothing about that narrative is verifiable. There is no council I might consult, no evidence to hold in my hands.

"Becoming a mother was my biggest ambition," my mother has told me more than once, and because we are so similar, because we were once onebody, I took that to mean that I too would be a mother. How could I be my mother's child if I was not going to be a mother myself? That would be a negation of her one true ambition. I sensed that if I could keep myself just this side of sane, I might make something useful out of the love I had inherited from my father. Having a child, making a person with my body, would be my one true creation. Where I failed on the page, I would flourish in life. What could be a more sensible, natural expression of my monstrous love? A way back to the beginning, our original, shared wonder. A life force to combat its encroaching shadow. A girl-child to ensure my mother would never die.

I lose my shit, there's no mistaking it, here on the bed beside my stalwart fiancé, this sensible man. Here, a plot twist I had not anticipated. There was a child and now, in an instant, there is not. There was one sort of life and now another. There was an ocean and now an absence. She was a vague outline, the smell of warm bananas on her breath, an echo down the hall. I saw her run and fall and smash ants with her fist. I heard her call to me in the night like a foghorn guiding a boat to shore. I felt her weight, compact and soft, and then lean and dense, our disparate features conflated on her perfect, bobbling head. I could taste the salt of her skin and feel the syllables of her name forming on my tongue. But he doesn't see her, so she doesn't exist. More certifiable is this: my truth doesn't exist and his does. The absence is the reality, no matter the wilds of my imagination. Here's my confession. I can go back over our time together, my personality, his, the texture and tenor of our relationship, and find a pattern that makes a kind of sense. If I squint, I can see it. It was always barreling toward us, this finality; it has always been.

Seeing him cry for the first time is mystifying. He hides his face between his knees. He shakes. It does not come naturally. The sounds are strained and awkward, like a body relearning an ancient trick. I want to comfort him, but my anger keeps me rooted. If ever there were a deal-breaker, this is it, and we both know it.

The wedding looms.
A shuttle driver named Lou.
Two gold rings purchased on the internet.
An arbor made from birch trees.

"I don't want to be a father, Jess," Jack says finally. "It's not going to happen."

When he looks at me, his expression red and melting, his eyes blazed with fear, I see exactly how long this confession has tormented him. I know that he doesn't know how or why he feels this way. But I am not calm like my protagonist. I do not behave with reason or patience or compassion. I am already in my post-apocalyptic future, barren, alone, mourning. I throw my book. I throw a tantrum. He holds his hands out to me and I smack them away like a child.

*   *   *   *   *

Only hours earlier, when becoming a family was still imminent, we'd been preparing to meet our friends Hannah and Greg for dinner at a Vietnamese restaurant around the corner. The bathroom window was opaque with rime and blooming ice fractals shaped like snowflakes. On the other side of the window, fog sifted through beams of light from streetlamps. Chimneys churned out smoke and the streets steamed. A roiling cold. A cliché setting for a confession. Jack had been sitting on the bed with his computer, absorbed in some rabbit hole of YouTube videos or antique auction sites or men's clothing stores. He frowned and clicked, chewing on his nails. He wore a thick flannel shirt cuffed neatly below the elbow and a pair of dark jeans and black socks. His chest rose and fell, and I watched the circle of soft, white skin just below his throat blink on and off in the light. I love that circle of skin, and all the tender places on his body. His collarbones, the backs of his knees, the tops of his feet. These are the places I like to kiss most, as if by doing so I cast a spell of protection around this beloved body. Watching him then, I was tempted to cancel our plans, avoid the tundra outside and instead slip beside him on the bed, finger that live spot on his throat, cover it with my mouth. But then he'd want to fuck and I wouldn't want to fuck. I was too hungry or bored or tired for that, though which combination thereof I couldn't say for sure. It's likely I'd had a headache, too, or a fever, or a hangnail. It's not that I don't enjoy fucking him, it's just that the whole process is more emotionally complicated for me than it is for Jack. It's not merely a physical act, but a whole physiological and spiritual journey. To have sex, and especially sex to orgasm, is to enter a hole of awe and terror. To counter bliss and grief. To slip into the stream of the collective unconscious and yet be forced back, time and time again. I didn't have my first orgasm until my late twenties, and when I did, I saw my dead father. I know, ridiculous, but it's true. I fell into the grief first, which I couldn't otherwise let myself feel, and then his face appeared just to ensure that my good time was ruined. Generally, I was too busy to grieve. To do so would have forced me to relinquish the cloak of achievement that I used as a shield against it. I had degrees to earn ("All those degrees gonna keep you warm at night?" my brother asked me once), jobs to acquire, books to write, a relationship to secure, a ravenous love-hunger to feed.

Over time, our sex together taught me to enter a space where I could approach that chasm of awe and not fall into it, and yet, it's not an easy thing for me. I can't just casually fuck on a Tuesday night.

So instead of canceling our dinner plans, I started to sing, badly, and he closed his computer and got up from the bed. On cue, he danced wildly and shook like Beyoncé. I slid behind him and slapped his butt, as if riding a bucking bronco. I rode him into the dining room where we danced around the table in a circle, a conga line of two. He bent over and touched the floor and I whooped, *oh, shit!*, then turned around and did the same. "Oh, shit!" he whooped. We stomped and howled and shimmied our chests at each other like preening birds.

"If you like it then you better put a ring on it!" I sang.
"If you like it then you better put a ring on it!" he sang.

We moved our hips in circles, stomped loudly, and waved our left hands in the air, my engagement ring glinting in the light. I put my arms around his neck and he kissed me quickly, stiffly, a pencil poke. "Don't pencil-poke me," I said. He sighed and kissed me again, this time with soft lips, the way I like it. It was time to go to dinner. It was nearly time to confess.

* * * * *

In the morning, my eyes are swollen and there's blood on both
our pillows. One of us is getting a bloody nose at night, but we're
not sure who since we swap pillows in our sleep. It's been below
twenty degrees outside for a week straight. We both have blue
faces and low dopamine levels. After Jack leaves for work, I run
errands instead of grading student essays. The grocery store
clerk scans and bags my cashews, butter pecan ice cream, and
Mexican-grown arugula, motions to the screen, and bangs at
her register. This winter, like the last four winters in Vermont,
I notice that the season silences people. Instead of expending
energy on casual conversation, we rely on alternative forms of
communication—grunting, nodding, gesturing—too despon-
dent for actual speech. If Vermont in summer is a lush and vir-
ile body, winter is the dark of her coffin. *Chilled to the bone*, they
say—the sun slams like a lid every afternoon at four. She's a tempestuous motherland. *She giveth and she taketh away.* That's how it
is until May. Nobody takes offense; this is survival mode.

What I don't know yet is this: there are four years before my
mother's diagnosis. In that time, the narrative of our lives will
change shape many times. Jack and I will marry and buy our
first home. We'll fight, make up, adopt a one-eyed dog. A year after our wedding, we'll spend three weeks in Spain on our honeymoon and upon our arrival make love in a strip of sunlight
inside the cheap room we'd rented, jet-lagged and jittery, before passing out for three hours on the floor. Because he gets angry when I ask him if he's enjoying himself, I won't, but I'll note
his impassive expression over steaming plates of paella, a dish
I'll try to replicate for him back home weeks later but ruin instead. Mid-honeymoon, I'll get a 103-degree fever and drag myself to the Prado anyway, sit on a bench in the middle of a gallery
in front of Antonio Gisbert's painting of the execution of José
María Torrijos, watching hazy, blindfolded figures blur together
and apart. We'll climb to the top of the Alhambra in Granada,

but when I turn around he won't be there. I'll find him later, still at the bottom, taking pictures of children carrying red balloons beside a steep cliff. Every night I'll insist that we go to flamenco, just so I can feel something in the dark. One night he'll go to bed at nine and I'll get drunk alone and wander the crowded streets of Córdoba awestruck by the ancient cobblestones and bow-legged cathedrals; the splayed and severed pig bodies hanging in shop windows; couples kissing between sips of wine; a solemn procession of young men floating down a winding back alley carrying a life-sized papier-mâché Jesus over their heads and following a stoic priest swinging a glinting, gold censer, slowly spilling smoke. They are trailed by a gaggle of children garbed in white gowns and singing softly, sifting through a veil of frankincense and myrrh. A smiling old man in a white apron, stained with blood, will wave me into his little empty bar, serve me a glass of velvety rioja and thick slices of sweet, peppery ham, then lock the door, grab my hair in his fist, bend my neck backward against the chair, and shove his tongue in my mouth. Later, I'll stumble into our room and sit in the dark watching Jack sleep for hours before finally curling into a ball atop a dusty futon mattress and passing out. The next morning, I log onto his computer to check on our dinner reservations and come across an email with the subject heading, "Hey baby, when's our next date?" What he says, roughly, is this: *I do not know her. It is just like porn, only live. It is not cheating. I was just curious.* He'll explain it away and I'll believe him because I need to believe him. A few days later, in the morning, after hours of walking the streets of Córdoba in cheap sandals that scraped away the skin on both my heels, he'll give me his sneakers and traipse the rest of the mile back in his socks while juggling sour oranges he'd plucked from a tree in the park. Later that afternoon, beneath hundreds of arching ocher vaults inside the Mosque of Córdoba, I'll feel a swell of swift dark pass over me like a storm. When I turn to him, face wet with tears, he'll stare back blankly, then raise his camera to his face. I freeze. He rarely takes my picture, so why now?

Fine, I think, fuck it. I stare back, feeling the tears hot on my face. I will not look away. But then he swivels to the left and snaps a picture of the floor tiles instead.

When he decides to move out a year later, as suddenly and un-flinchingly as he'd snapped that photo, I'll lock myself in the house for four months, leaving only to teach and go to the grocery store, making and remaking paella night after night, trying to perfect the spongy consistency of the rice, the delicate balance of salt, spice, and saffron, the mix of seafood and sausage—only to dump the whole dish in the trash every time.

But this is all still in the future.

Today, a Tuesday in December of 2014, I silently exchange funds with the grocery store clerk—my paper, her coins—and exit without a word. In the parking lot, I spot a place called *Body Le Bronze* and impulsively pay fifteen dollars for seven minutes in a tanning booth, just to feel heat on my skin. When I return home in the afternoon, Lucille is walking down the street in her enormous, pale blue overcoat and pushing a rickety baby carriage, its left rear wheel spinning in circles. We're not sure where she lives, but every day Lucille passes by our apartment in the overcoat, pushing the stroller, head down and determined. Today she is shuffling; the plastic bag that she fills with other plastic bags collected from the grocery store is stuffed to capacity. She wears a pair of rubber Nike sandals over two different socks, one red, one white, and when the wind blows, her long, gray hair lifts in the back like a cape.

"Hi, Lucille," I say.
"Trash!" she screams, pointing at my face. "Trash!"

Then she hands me one of her plastic grocery bags and tucks the rest back into the stroller, pulling a blanket over her parcel and patting it gently. As she continues down the street, one of the neighbor boys appears behind me. The poet, sandy-haired and tall. He puts a bag of trash in the trash can and walks over to me. We stand there together on the driveway for a moment, watching Lucille disappear around the corner, a single plastic bag blowing behind her like a tumbleweed.

[THE DEAD PARENTS CLUB]

I.

The four of us met in college more than fifteen years ago. Hannah, her (now) husband, Greg, and I were all in the same writing class. Jack and I lived in the same dorm. They still tease me about the white Chanel loafers I wore back then, a gift from my grandmother, and the most expensive thing I'd ever owned. I didn't know three-hundred-dollar shoes existed. Secretly, I'd sensed they were ugly, but hoped they were cool by association alone. Maybe I just wasn't sophisticated enough to recognize their high-end beauty, but surely my fellow undergrads were wowed by the gold, interlocking C's, the fine point of the toe, the buttery leather. "We were not," Hannah says now, rubbing her chopsticks together. It is three hours before Jack's confession and we're having dinner together at our favorite restaurant, which is exactly halfway between our two homes in Winooski. It is two years before Jack and I buy a house and move to Waterbury.

All these years after college and we all live in the same town again. Hannah and I are thrilled; Greg is happy; and Jack would prefer otherwise. He likes them just fine, but really, his introversion is cresting to a point of inflection, though neither of us know it yet. The restaurant is one of those hole-in-the-wall hidden gems—a Vietnamese place that serves outrageous portions of fragrant noodles, fresh vegetables, and a choice of one of three proteins, all on the cheap. Hannah and Greg have recently returned from a trip to Turkey, during which they walked in the cold rain for a week. Greg cracks open a large, hoppy beer in a can as colorful as a Dali painting. He takes a large swig, inhales sharply through his nose, then rubs both hands over his face. Hannah pulls out a brown paper bag out of which she retrieves a souvenir ashtray glazed in blood orange swirls. I don't tell her that I'll be giving up smoking soon, since I want to get pregnant after the wedding. Jack and I haven't talked about having kids in a while, but I think we'll do it soon. We've always treated the topic like a benign inevitability, like something we know is expected of us and that we'll get around to eventually. I haven't yet shared with Jack the rapturous desire for a child I've been experiencing in the last few months. I don't quite trust the feeling, and so speaking it aloud feels premature. Greg pours soy sauce in the ashtray and begins dipping his tofu in it.

I thank Hannah and kiss her hard on the mouth, which is something we've only started doing recently, since we all befriended the couple across the street from us who kiss everyone on the mouth. Suddenly, all our friends kiss one another on the mouth. I love this new development. I love kissing people on the mouth, especially women, whose lips are plump and soft and never pursed as if in constipation like Jack's lips. Some days, I have to refrain from kissing everyone on the mouth: strangers, students, Lucille, the man who works at the corner Sunoco and gave me a free coffee on my way to work the other morning because I looked "sad as dirty snow."

I like Greg's odd habits, like the way he insists on eating all of one item on his plate before proceeding to another, for example, and the matter-of-fact way he relates to his own strange behaviors. They make sense to him, so he doesn't feel compelled to defend himself when we tease him. Occasionally, in the middle of dinner, he'll get up and go take a walk around the block. Or he'll stay up until three in the morning playing video games while eating an entire box of cereal out of a mixing bowl. Or, once, on a group trip to the Maine coast, he spent an entire morning using a blow-up lounge chair as a makeshift boat, paddling with his long arms and legs between various nearby rock islands, maybe half a mile between each one, as if manning a more seaworthy vessel. This was not an ironic gesture. His face revealed his intensity. We watched him from the porch of the cottage we'd rented, laughing and conjecturing.

"Where's Gilligan headed now?"
"Ahoy, matey! Your siren waits upon these shores!"
"Um, is he going to make it back on that thing?"
When we questioned him about it later, he'd scoffed.
"What? It worked, didn't it?"

Worked for what, we weren't sure, but he only shrugged, cracked a beer, and smiled tepidly at the sea.

When we were young, the three of us—Hannah, Greg, and me—bonded over grief. The Dead Parents Club, we called ourselves. Even at eighteen, I unknowingly gravitated toward people who'd suffered some sort of trauma or another. As if Loss was a shared homeland, lush, volcanic, and shaped like a poem. From the shores of Loss we could see great distances. We dined on the fruits of Loss and eyed her waters for signs of incoming wreckage. On Loss, we grew up wary but grateful for small things. Every time we dug our hands into the cool sands, or watched the birds circle overhead, or tasted the sweat on someone else's skin, we marveled. We marveled too at the barren trees, the shallows, and the carcasses tossed carelessly into early graves. Loss is a contradictory homeland, and therefore rife with wonders.

Hannah's mother, Jane, died in a car accident when Hannah was four years old. Hannah was in the car, as were her two younger brothers, Hector and Caleb. Of that day, and her mother in general, Hannah remembers very little. "I remember being upset that they cut my dress off at the hospital. It was my favorite dress," she told me the first night we met—after our mutual professor had pushed us together at a bar post-class. "Here," he'd said, "you two should talk. You both have a dead parent," as if this alone ensured our compatibility. Then he'd turned and climbed onto the small stage in the back of the bar, tossed a feather boa over his shoulder, and began singing a baroque adaptation of "Lola" into a gold-plated microphone.

But he was right, it did unite us. We were both a little graver than our peers, a little more cynical and spirited. We drank a lot, and smoked, and made fun of a girl named Rebecca who took herself too seriously but only wanted to be our friend. She moped in the corner one night while Hannah and I giggled in her single bed, passing a flask of whiskey back and forth. To this day, we don't feel bad about it, although we probably should. Greg and I both lost our fathers shortly before arriving at college. Greg's dad suffered a sudden heart attack. My father drank a pint of vodka, had a grand mal seizure, and fell down a flight of stairs. I love Greg's mother, Maureen, who has a broad, square face, a blunt, blonde bob, and the deep voice of a radio personality. She is warm and maternal. When she visits, I have to make a deliberate effort not to crawl into her lap. Not to kiss her on the mouth.

That Jack hasn't suffered a major loss yet is not relevant to his impending disappearance. He will suffer one soon, and what it shifts in him will remain a mystery to the rest of us.

After Jane died, Hannah's dad, Colin, raised the kids alone for a while. He bought a home in Burlington and started his own house painting business. Later, he remarried and had a fourth child: Given. They have become like a second family to Jack and me since we moved to Vermont. Colin is a short, bald, big-bellied eccentric who bears a striking resemblance to Wallace Shawn, the character actor perhaps best known for his role as Vizzini in *The Princess Bride* or Wallace in *My Dinner with Andre.*

Colin also has excellent taste in food and wine and often wears a beret unironically, or instead his "ham hat," a twenty-year-old cloth bag that once contained an Easter ham and now hangs on a hook in his kitchen for whenever the mood strikes. He often invites us over for elaborate meals, during which we sit around his dining room table alit with candles—Jack, Hannah, Greg, Hannah's brothers, and me—while he tells us stories about the old neighborhood or explains again why he keeps his pot in the safety deposit box at the bank, lest he risk smoking it all in one sitting. Once, he asked me to score him some, which I did, eager to return his generosity, but he was incredulous at the amount I'd managed to procure. "What's this supposed to be?" he said, pinching the tiny baggie between his thumb and forefinger. "An appetizer?"

Over dinner at the Vietnamese place, the night of Jack's confession ("I don't want to be a father. Not ever."), Hannah shows us a picture on her phone of her school lunch from thirty years ago: a calcified apple, a bagel sandwich wrapped in tinfoil, and a copy of a reading report that apparently never made it to the teacher. Colin had recently found the old lunch bag in the basement, tucked behind some duct work. According to her reading report, Hannah had really loved *A Tree Grows in Brooklyn*, but Colin insists she'd forged his signature. "If I had a baby, I'd name it Nolan after the main character," she says, but everyone knows she doesn't want a baby. She's adamant about this. For a brief time, Greg had been disappointed, but he came around to the idea and now he's quite pleased with it.

I imagine Jane.

I imagine her buckling her three, small children into the back seat of her sedan. It is a warm summer morning in 1988. Setting off into the mist, the kids whine and kick. The youngest, Caleb, soon falls asleep in his car seat, his melon face tipped to his chest. I imagine it's dawn and the moon is still as bright as an iceberg in a sea of pale, devotional blue. As they coast down I-89, splitting the sea in a small, brown Pontiac Tempest, Hall & Oates is on the tape player and the passenger window is wide open. The loud wind calms the older kids, so that by the time the truck's single headlight appears through the gauzy clouds ahead, they are quiet and drowsy, listening to "Sara Smile" float in and out of an endless wind tunnel. Why this fantasy persists is a mystery to me. After all, it's not my story, and this version I tell myself is entirely false, a hackneyed construction made out of scrap metal and piecemeal information. My obsession with Jane's final day haunts me more than it should, and I keep it a secret. In part, it feels wrapped up in the love I have for Hannah, as if by conjuring her mother's ghost, I might learn to love my friend better. As if by reliving this fantasy I privately honor her mother, thanking her again and again for gifting me her small girl-child with her crooked nose and quiet, persistent friendship. My sister in love and loss. But creating my friend and then dying young were not Jane's imperatives; nor did my mother set out to give birth to an addict. These women were artists, crafting their own lives out of whatever materials they had at hand. In this way, we're all scrap artists, begging, borrowing, stealing from one another as we cobble together a life worth living. Worth honoring. We are all source material, and each of us an epic.

Jane had been a potter and at Hannah's wedding, one of Jane's friends gave her a set of her mother's bowls. "She'd want you to have them," the friend had said. "I saved them for you all these years." When I look at the bowls now, stacked neatly on open shelves in Hannah's kitchen, delicate and old, I try to fit them into a narrative about destiny and randomness. About Loss as a land of beautiful artifacts and thirty-year-old calcified lunches. About love as inheritance and willful action. About Jane and the driver of that semi-truck having always been en route to one another—careening in slow motion, over miles and years. If you ask Hannah if her mother's absence influenced her decision not to become a mother, she'll only shrug. "Maybe," she'll say. "And maybe not." To revise our self-narratives is not a luxury but a survival tool. If Eric ever gets sober it will be because he lived a life that was always in support of that conclusion. If he doesn't, the same will be true. Only the shape of the story shifts with time. I want to be able to look down and see a shape for my life that does not contain a body made from my body. I want that shape to be as full as the one that contains that body. And since language is story's material, then here is my revision.

*　*　*　*　*

It's been a week since Jack's confession. We haven't talked about it since. I cannot rewrite our narrative so quickly, so instead I say nothing. It's Friday. Our new friends, the couple who live across the street, Kara and Rya, come over for dinner. We kiss them on the mouth and sit at the table like the adults we have mysteriously become. Because they are vegetarians, I've made something that resembles bean mash. I found the recipe in one of my grandmother's old cookbooks, which shows how much I know about vegetarian cuisine. In the kitchen, Jack and I move around one another gingerly, then silently bring dishes out to the table where our friends are drinking wine and smiling impishly. They pick at the meal politely, slicing off chunks of bread and helping themselves to extra olives. After dinner, we move to the living room for more wine. I can't look at Jack but feel him move around me like a pocket of heat. When he gets up my chest clenches. His confession has revealed to me an unpredictability I'd never noticed before. He could be capable of anything now. Square dancing. Pissing on the floor. Speaking in tongues. Who knows? Who is this guy, anyway, and how did he get into my apartment? Much of what I love about Jack is his predictability—a steadiness I didn't have growing up. He never drinks too much and falls down the stairs. He does not need to find himself inside the dark recesses of bars and strange women. His needs have always seemed relatively straightforward: food, sex, alone time, quiet labors like building furniture, painting, and gardening.

As our years together accumulated, there was never a time when the question of parenthood seemed suddenly prudent. Why discuss it today as opposed to yesterday? We were nineteen, twenty, twenty-one. We were in college and then graduate school. New jobs and ever more U-Hauls that needed packing. In the end, though, there is no good excuse for why we left this conversation unspoken. We just did.

"We want to get pregnant," Kara announces. "Rya's thirty-five, so ya know." They smile at each other and sip their wine. I drain my glass, stand, and head into the kitchen for a new bottle. "But, um, obviously we'll need a sperm donor."

"Well, shit, we need to celebrate!" I call back. I realize now that I'm a little drunk. It strikes me as miraculous that anyone could be so sure of anything. But how do you really know? I want to ask them. What if you regret it? Why now and not, say, next year? The year after? Just what the fuck are we doing here? Is this the point? I want to ask them. Somebody please tell me what I'm supposed to be doing.

Rya will carry the baby, they tell us when I get back with the booze. Though the younger of the two, Kara has the gene for cystic fibrosis. Her twin sister died from the disease when they were eighteen. She starts many sentences with *Once, on a Make-a-Wish trip* . . . which previously I had only ever imagined to be some sort of elaborate nineties hoax. I drive the corkscrew deeper into the cork and start to laugh. Here it comes, I think. "What an honor!" I'll say when they ask Jack to be the donor. I practice beaming beatifically while I pry the cork out of the bottle. "I don't see why not! Jack?" And then I'll sit there smiling maniacally while he shits himself.

"We're thinking about asking Greg," says Rya, then takes a sip
of wine. Jack is leaning forward on the couch, his elbows on his
knees, his face as pale as the sauvignon blanc he hasn't touched.

* * * * *

In our early twenties I had envisioned our years together as the
maiden voyage of a lifelong adventure. Now I remember those
years as the first in a series of bedding-downs, designed to help
each of us reach this place where we can finally procreate and
feign adulthood like the rest of them. In our early twenties, I'd
thought we would travel the world, collecting odd jobs and stories. Now my college students tell me how they will travel the
world, collecting odd jobs and stories. Once I thought we'd make
art and take drugs. Now I want to make people and take probiotics. They are irreconcilable, these two disparate life stories. To
deal with this problem, I stick ruthlessly to a present tense, both
in life and in writing. Otherwise, I'm left with narratives like
this one, which can't be trusted.

The first time I held an infant in my arms I was eleven years old.
My mother had offered me up to watch the son of a client while
they toured the woman's home and my mother advised her on
preparing the property for sale. "She's wonderful with babies,"
she told the woman when we arrived, and I'd nodded dumbly,
terrified.

The child was five months old and large for his age. He had
cloudy, blue eyes and a puckered chin and took my pinky finger
into his wet mouth with a quick shake of his head. He could roll
from his back to his stomach and eat mashed vegetables, though
I didn't know that at the time. I held him in my arms and paced
the living room. He was a marvel, intoxicating. We danced in
circles, my feet gliding easily on the parquet floor. He was warm
and heavy, heavier than I had expected. I could hear my mother

down the hall speaking to the baby's mother in her realtor voice, making up something about fêng shui. She had a habit of speaking authoritatively on subjects she only vaguely understood. I didn't know it then, but this is a habit most adults share: this need to seem well-versed in something, anything, and how such deceptions are a comfort over a lifetime of small failures. Then, I just thought my mother was a liar.

I sat down on the sofa with the child in my arms. I do not remember his name, though I remember lifting him to my flat chest and watching with wonder as he suckled the fabric of my sweatshirt, his jaw working mechanically, and then the little yelp of frustration as he realized the truth about me: I was a monkey made of cloth and wire. The child simpered, and I tried to put my pinky back in his mouth, but by then it was too late.

Down the hall, the women laughed, and bedroom doors opened and banged shut. "Wallpaper," I heard my mother say. "Neutral colors."

I laid the child on the sofa. He had lost his sheen. He mewled and rubbed his nose with his doughy fists. I covered him gently in his white blanket and moved toward the hallway to find someone else to do the job.

I must not have been looking when he tumbled the three feet from the sofa to the floor, because I remember the sound of his skull thumping twice, and it was as strange a sound as I had ever heard. I remember his white blanket open and empty and draped over the edge of the sofa cushion. I remember thinking about an unspooled cocoon, and the way a moth will slowly beat its black wings in the sunshine for long minutes before evaporating into the sky. I remember scooping up the child and staring into his face and silently begging him to cry. I remember feeling euphoric with new purpose. Instead of crying, he stared, his blue eyes blank and wide, his mouth a cavern of silence. I shook him gently, *cry*, and his chest rose and he took a deep audible breath and bellowed, *unholy sound*, bellowed into my face.

My mother appeared and I told her everything, that I had been walking with the baby in my arms and tripped over the edge of the sofa, catching myself before I fell, but the baby, poor nameless baby I would never see again, had been startled by the sound.

"I didn't let him go," I said. "Thank goodness I didn't let him go."

I'm not sure why this memory with the infant persists. I know only that it's wrapped up with two conflicting ideas of myself—that I would be a terrific mother and a very bad one—and it changes all the time.

* * * * *

The truth is I am envious of Hannah's desirelessness, which seems to me now a great freedom. Wouldn't I rather spend my days writing instead of childrearing? Wouldn't I rather travel and grow wise with worldly experience? Do I not value my autonomy to come and go as I please? To follow my impulses with impunity? Is this not the pinnacle of gender equality—a partner who does not value me as a mere conduit for his legacy? A nursemaid for his heirs? For most of human history, a woman's primary function was the birthing of more men. And if not a male child, then at least a female who would then give birth to a male. Women were not considered whole unto themselves. No wonder we are still trying to fill our holes. A daughter's inherited truth is partly the knowledge that she is not finished *becoming* until she is a mother. At which point she is simply finished, meant to spend her days nurturing and raising that child, and then quietly ushered back into the pastures whence she came.

*   *   *   *   *

"I like my life the way it is," Jack says finally.

I've laid out our options like so many hands of rummy:
Either we marry or we do not marry.
Either we decide on children now or later.
Either we trust ourselves to come to a decision together or we do not.

"I like our apartment, the quiet. I like it clean. I like that we can travel whenever we want."

"We don't travel," I remind him. "That involves interacting with other humans and you don't do that."

"I want a dog," he says.

"All misanthropes want dogs."

He reddens, the flush flaring from his neck beneath his thickening beard and over the rise of his cheekbones. I like to kiss him there, on the two tender swells beneath his eyes where he burns like a boy in the summers. "I interact with humans all day. Why shouldn't I spend my evenings alone?" I know that if I press that button he'll insist, again, that he doesn't mean *me*. He likes having *me* around. I am the only one he can happily endure for more than mere minutes. It's always made me feel strangely proud, that I managed to invade his bubble of reproach before it hardened into this implacable shell.

He's always been introverted, exhausted by the company of friends. I cosign his excuses: another late night at work, the mysterious illnesses, his father's weeks-long recovery from shoulder surgery, seemingly valid reasons he can't make this event or that. Eventually, I learn to prefer seeing our friends without him.

[THE DEAD PARENTS CLUB]
134

Easier to enjoy myself without his quiet discomfort. Just one of those compromises of relationships, I figure.

Then, finally, "What if you give birth to an addict?" but he says it so quickly and quietly I'm not sure I've heard it at all.

* * * * *

If women baffle Jack, men are intolerable—the gulfs of silence between men rattle him most of all. Women fill empty space, at least, with their bodies if not their opinions. They are mountains to be navigated, foraged, and weathered. But he is a joy to be with, once he resolves to grace you with his company. He will be funny, polite, and solicitous. He is beloved by my family and our friends, even if he privately doesn't share in their affection. "Are you hungry?" he asks our guests. "Thirsty? Let me fill your glass?" he says. *Oh, go on, have another.* Our friends fling their irony across rooms like peas. They drink too much. They max out credit cards. Jack drinks orange juice and watches, waiting for them to leave.

Occasionally, they marry and have children, and it changes nothing and everything.

"It exhausts me. It takes all of my energy. I need the next few weekends to myself," Jack often says after an evening with company.

I can't help but take it personally, as if I have failed to find the right sort of company, as if I too am not the right sort of company, since each of our friends mirror some facet of my own personality, my sense of irony and goodwill and creativity and grief and gluttony. Aren't we all just fractured versions of one another? Don't we seek out company to remind ourselves of our own humanity? Lest we end up talking nonsense to the gulls?

And yet, despite all our years together, I still underestimate the terror he feels when he imagines another being occupying our space. It isn't the work or the money or the sleepless nights he fears the most, it is the inherent obligation to entertain, the fear of being outed for his social discomfort, which he works so hard to hide. It is the inability to fully show up for another person. To be present in a selfless way. I've even tried joking that a child will make the perfect excuse for him to stay in.

Or. Long after it's posed, I hear his question hanging in the air.

What if you give birth to an addict?

And suddenly my body is incriminated, charged with a crime it has not yet committed.

*   *   *   *   *

Greg and Hannah consider donating Greg's sperm to Kara and Rya. They say *maybe*, then *yes*. I try to envision this child, a genetic mash-up of my two friends: dark-haired, olive-skinned, tall or short, thin probably, brown eyes. I want to imagine that Rya and Kara's child will be *our* child. We'll raise her together in a hippie utopia. She'll move freely between our three homes and never knock, showing up with her school bag and peanut butter and jelly crusts, homework that needs correcting, a paper cut that needs bandaging. She'll ask for snacks and hugs and we'll give her slices of cheese and pepperoni, a treat her vegetarian moms don't forbid but won't condone either. We'll all be on the call list at school and I'll pick her up when she's sick in the nurse's office, since I have the most flexible work schedule, and drop her off at Hannah and Greg's while I hit the gym for an hour, and then Kara or Rya will pick her up after work. (In this fantasy, I am impossibly fit and beautiful because, having never birthed my own child, I have ample time for exercise and facials.)

But the longer I indulge this fantasy, the more unrealistic it seems. And the longer they discuss it—Rya, Kara, Hannah, and Greg—the more unrealistic it becomes. Ultimately, Kara and Rya choose to shoulder the expense of a sperm donor. It's less complicated, in the end. During our usual Saturday night get-togethers, they start to temper their wine consumption so that by 9 p.m. Kara can inject Rya with the hormones necessary to prepare her body for intrauterine insemination. The hormones make her tired and the injections are unpleasant, but they keep at it. They share with us the spec sheets for the prospective donors. They read like dating profiles, except here the stakes seem impossibly high. They can't unmake this choice or break up with it when it disappoints them. An exaggeration could be life changing. A lie could be fatal. We cringe and make worried faces at one another. We read snippets aloud and make uninformed judgments.

6'1", blond hair, brown eyes, 180 lbs. 24 years old at time of donation. No history of drug use. Non-smoker. Social drinker. Republican. Methodist. Plays piano and soccer. 3.75 GPA in high school. No college. Reads poetry and prefers virtual reality. Likes: Xbox, skiing, golf, water sports, airplanes. Maternal grandfather has a heart condition, otherwise no known genetic conditions. One uncle on the father's side is an alcoholic but died before the donor was born. Would permit contact after child turns 18 years old.

5'11", brown hair, brown eyes, 176 lbs. Muscular body type. 21 years old at time of donation. No history of drug use. Non-smoker. Non-drinker. No political or religious affiliations. A history major. Wants to be a high school teacher. 3.42 GPA in high school. Current GPA: 2.89. Likes: George Washington, the Denver Broncos, Chinese food, and martial arts. No family history of addiction or genetic diseases. One gay uncle. No contact desired.

5'2", brown hair, blue eyes, 142 lbs. 41 years old at time of donation. Some history of drug use. Social smoker. Social drinker. No political or *religious affiliations. Phlebotomist. GPAs unknown. Likes: cars, robotics, Star Wars, cooking, and jazz music. Some family history of addiction and male-pattern baldness. Two uncles in the Ku Klux Klan. Would permit contact after child turns 18 years old. *Donor does not agree with the KKK agenda; his niece is half-black.*

Kara hands me another one and waits while I read it.

"He's a writer," she says. "We like him."

We're sitting at their kitchen table on a Sunday morning, trading donor profiles back and forth like playing cards. "Listen to this one," says Jack. "This guy likes denim overalls and slot machines."

"I have a cousin who's a KISS fan," Rya says, tossing aside another profile. "He's just okay."

Most of the donors are college students making extra cash. I wonder if any of them envision the children their sperm will help create, and if they too will like Chinese food, have a cleft chin, and prefer boxers to briefs. I wonder if they imagine raising kids one day, or if donating sperm is a way to extend their genetic legacy while also eschewing parental responsibility. Reading through the profiles, I also feel a voyeuristic thrill. It reminds me of Edmund Burke's essay on the sublime, in which he explains how humans thrill at fear from a safe distance. I want to know more about these guys. I want pictures and links to their Facebook profiles. Mother's maiden names and stories about dead pets and corny uncles. I want to know about their ambitions. *Look me in the eye*, I want to say. I want these men to walk into this kitchen right now and tell me if they can handle fatherhood for real one day. If this sperm donation thing is just a fucking means to an end—tuition, gas money, another Xbox game. If they've thought it through to its natural conclusion. If they're sure.

"OK, well, we have to pay extra to ask questions," says Kara, "so can we work with what we have here?" And they are, aren't they? Working. Creating. Making something out of nothing. Manifesting a body out of a shared love for the world. The invisible work that most straight couples do to make a child is for Kara and Rya not only more difficult and expensive, but also testament to the process of art-making. I once heard someone say that the pain of grief is equal to the worth of the love we grieve. But for Kara and Rya, and anyone who struggles to get pregnant, and all women artists engaged with the wonder of creation of any kind, the cost is commensurate with the sine qua non.

When I look up again Jack is gone, out back playing fetch with the couple's golden retriever, tossing the ball high into the air, his left shoe untied. As I watch him, I feel a shocking sense of betrayal, except I've realized it too late. Jack is not just disinterested in making a family with me; he is busy working out how to escape the one we've already created.

*   *   *   *   *

It is May now, and Vermont spins silently toward spring. Jack and I put the conversation in a drawer; pull the dress from the closet. It comes down to this: *we are not ready to be apart*. We've grown up together these last twelve years, and it would be uselessly reductive to say we've grown apart. The truth is, we've grown together and apart, and our devotion is not a mistake, exactly. It just is. If we were able to predict what came next, the rage and pain, would we still get married? Well, it doesn't matter, does it? And if one day I give birth to a child who grows into addiction? I will love that child as ferociously as my mother loves her son. And we will suffer too. And it will all be part of my private wonder. I give myself over to it. I surrender to this essential condition, this bottomless embrace of terror and awe. I accept the consequences, as mothers and artists must in this visceral, primal pursuit of unachievable wholeness. I watch Jack from the window in front of my desk. He coaxes wire fencing around the posts of our garden. He threads the vines of a new tomato plant through the holes in the fencing. The vine droops, then finds its bearings and hovers in the sun. Jack packs the soil tightly near the roots, then stands and holds his arms out wide, waiting. He turns and sees me watching from the window and smiles, slaps dirt from his hands, beckons me out. "Look," he says, pointing to the tomato plant. And maybe because the earth has shifted on her axis, however slightly, or because my blue delphinium has finally let down her hair. Or because the tomato plant nods and the mountains are moored in the distance, or because we have just eaten a good meal and the light is low. Or perhaps it is because, despite myself, I am writing the novel I am no longer trying and failing to write. For all of these reasons or none of them, I sense her floating there between us: little spacewalker, my necessary fiction.

And just like that, I've revised my story. Now she's a ghost. She's the pouring glory of the world. I can see her whenever I want. Language is magic, after all.

"Yes," I say. "I'm looking."

II.

Two years later.

After months of hormone therapy, surgery to remove a benign cyst on her uterus, five ineffectual rounds of intrauterine insemination, Rya and Kara begin the process of in vitro fertilization. They decide to stick with The Writer and I am not-so-secretly delighted. Rya's eggs are extracted and inseminated in several petri dishes. They wait for a call from the doctor saying that an embryo, or ideally more than one embryo, has begun to develop. We discuss the process extensively over weekend dinners: Jack and me, Hannah and Greg, Rya and Kara. We are hopeful, but also guarded. Artificial insemination had not been successful, and it had taken a toll on them. The odds of getting pregnant during a single round of artificial insemination are about 15 percent, similar to the odds of getting pregnant during a single round of unprotected, heterosexual sex. The odds of getting pregnant during a single round of in vitro fertilization are better—about 32 percent for women over thirty-five like Rya, but still not great.

And while rounds of artificial insemination had not yielded a pregnancy for Kara and Rya, innumerable rounds of unprotected sex had not yielded a pregnancy for Jessie and Jon (including one memorable session during which I accidentally interrupted, stumbling into their bedroom one night after a party, attempting to take up my rightful place beside Jessie in the bed). Zero rounds of unprotected heterosexual sex (to say nothing of the protected variety) had not yielded a pregnancy for Jack and me, though that was expected.

We have been married for two years now and are yet to discuss it again. The ghost-child follows us through the house, taking up space, and we tiptoe around her. One day I will decide. In that future, I will have a child with him, without him, or not at all. What I know is that I have the choice, and that is both a power and a burden. Many days, I do not feel a need for children. On these days, I feel a rush of gratitude for the freedom to make decisions about my life and career that are not dependent on putting someone else's needs first.

Is it the child herself, or the need to make something of this love, that haunts me? Is it the child herself, or the aching desire to give shape to this tremulous wonder? This ability to choose motherhood, or not choose motherhood, is a modern luxury that many women still don't have. I do not take it for granted. It is a privilege to ask these questions. It doesn't make them hurt less.

"You're not going to have a choice forever," my mother says. "Tick tock." She knows a woman who paid for her daughter to have her eggs frozen at thirty-two, and then the daughter gave birth at forty. Can I believe it? She offers to pay to have my eggs frozen, though I'd rather she put that money into her dwindling retirement fund. "Are you mad at me for suggesting it?" she wants to know. The woman's daughter was mad at her initially. I balk, laugh, and then finally agree to talk to my gynecologist about it. I cannot decide if this is an abuse of privilege, a modern marvel, or both. Can I buy immortality after all? On days when I desire a child more than food or sex or air, all ethical considerations evaporate; I don't give a shit. This is when I feel most animal, most purely human. I could bellow over these quiet, suburban streets, lash mountains with my sharp tongue, unhinge my bones from their sockets. I could tear holes in the fabric of the universe with nothing more than a hammer and my rage. This is what the fertility industry banks on, this primal imperative. This calling.

For some women, the call never comes. They are called elsewhere. To service or art or business or travel or a million other ways to expend their energy. Could I take these two hands, this harried brain, this gifted but finite store of energy and do both?

In her memoir about becoming a mother for the first time, Rachel Cusk writes, "I often think that people wouldn't have children if they knew what it was really like, and I wonder whether as a gender we contain a Darwinian stop upon our powers of expression, our ability to render the truth of this subject." I can anticipate how much I would hate the dailyness of motherhood—the waking, dressing, crying, shitting, pissing, vomiting, travel-inhibiting, terror-inducing slog of it—and yet still long for it. There is so much to fear: postpartum depression (I am a prime candidate), isolation from friends and family, Jack's

resentment, my own, the thousand daily boredoms of motherhood, those terrible songs and clacking toys, the piercing, soul-
sucking screams in the night.

"Your generation is brand new," my mother says. "You have all of
these choices. You're marrying later, if at all. You're having kids
later, if at all. It's nice, isn't it, except that you have to make it up
as you go. There's no precedent for your generation. Not really."

When we were kids in the eighties and nineties, my friends
and I watched our middle-class mothers try and fail to "have
it all." They worked, got divorced, and parented solo. Or they
went to therapy and stayed married until the kids graduated
from high school. They wore shoulder pads and negotiated
raises. They could always do better and more: at work, on the
PTA, shuttling us from practice to practice, cooking, cleaning,
dressing the part. We watched as they bought, broke, and lost
lipsticks. Tried Tae Bo and stopped after a week. Spilled coffee on their cheap pumps and never picked up the dry cleaning. Drank wine for dinner and ate the kids' leftovers for breakfast. Ignored school secretaries who frowned when they were
late picking us up. Accommodated or didn't husbands who
weren't quite ready to give up dinner at six. Ordered pizzas and
cried in the car. When the kids fought, our mothers lost their
shit; every straw was their last. New drugs were invented (Xanax! Ativan!) because America is nothing if not supportive of
the modern woman. Some mothers pinched their kids' Ritalin
prescriptions and vacuumed for hours on a Saturday morning.
Minivans were supposed to be a gift—*look how much room!*—
but ended up being just another space for mothers to clean. In
my town, rumors held that some kids had fathers at home, but
I didn't see many. Nearly all my friends were raised by single,
divorced mothers. This, we were told, is progress. It was meant
to be a lesson and it was.

No wonder we're skeptical. No wonder we looked side-eyed at the prospect of motherhood. No wonder we stare down time and test our bodies' resilience. Nurture our ambivalence and fear for our futures. Freeze our eggs and foster our creativity. We are making it up. We imagine and reimagine. Capitulate and doubt. We were taught to believe that everything we ever wanted awaited us, but we needed only look around to know how wrong that was.

Then one day the call comes. We pack our bags. We go.

*   *   *   *   *

I visit my mother in Pennsylvania for her fifty-eighth birthday. I bring the one-eyed dog and a case of Vermont beer for Jon, because everybody knows that Vermont beer is the best beer. I make dinner and Jessie and Jon arrive with dessert and a bottle of wine wrapped in tissue paper. "Open this one first," Jessie says, and hands it to me.

I unwrap the tissue paper but can't understand what I'm seeing. Glued to the bottle of wine are tiny, pink piglets made of what? Rubber? Candy? I look at her and she smiles all goofy. "What the fuck is that?" I say. I squint and turn the bottle around in my hands. They are not piglets but babies. Miniature, plastic, human babies—naked, pink, curled, and faceless—like something you might buy at a craft story to play Jesus in a tabletop nativity scene, or stuff inside a piñata at a baby shower, or use as a prop during a Halloween gag.

On the video that Jon is surreptitiously recording, I stumble backward holding the bottle of wine.

"No," I keep repeating, not because I am not happy, but because I am in shock. "No," I say. "No." But I am also crying, and then Jessie is crying, and then we are hugging and both crying, and in the background, Jon is laughing and saying *Awww.* "Well, there are a lot of complicated emotions going on here," my mother says sagely, then sighs and extracts a cigarette from her pack on the counter. Then, the video ends.

Suddenly, everyone's pregnant. Jessie and Jon in Pennsylvania. Rya and Kara here in Vermont. Sean and his beautiful wife, Sarah, have recently given birth to a daughter they name Winter. The whole internet, too, is pregnant. Blue and pink balloons festoon every photo on every social media platform.

There she is: little spacewalker. A girl-child Kara and Rya will name Maven. We squint to make out the shape of her on the ultrasound image on Kara's cell phone. She is a twirl of darkness against a backdrop of white, a shape shifter whose growth is measured in fruits and vegetables. She is a pea, a strawberry, a kumquat. When she finally morphs into a lime, her mothers relax a little. There—her fingers and toes, opening and closing. Eyes like smooth, black seeds. Intestines curl inside the abdominal wall. Two impossibly tiny ears like budding leaves, furred and unfurling, anoint either side of her delicate skull. Look— her whorling, dervish brain.

Days later, a similar image appears on my cell phone, a text from Jessie, except the clump of cells is the size of a blueberry still, a pinprick in a storm of white.

"I hope it's a boy," she writes.
"I know it's a boy," I write back.

Their respective due dates are only a few weeks apart, Jessie and Rya. We compare their basketed produce constantly.
Jessie's a grape this week!
Rya is a peach!
Jessie is a peach!
Rya is a cucumber!
I like this game a lot.

I threaten to eat both babies after they are born. I want to chew their fleshy thighs; grill and butter their toes like sweet corn; nibble their sweet rosebud mouths.

In April of 2017, Jack and I take a short trip to Asheville, North Carolina, where we'd lived for a year shortly after college. For two days, we walk the town inside a cloud of nostalgia. Time becomes fuzzy. Had we ever left? Had we not just yesterday eaten po' boys at Red's Diner, walked the wet banks of the French Broad River, squinted at the Blue Mountains? As we pass by Mayfel's, where I used to waitress, the same patio tables are draped in the same red and white checkered tablecloths, and I stare at the door waiting for my twenty-five-year-old self to walk out bearing plates of shrimp and grits. I can still smell the walk-in refrigerator where my friend Holly once pressed me against the rack of side salads and kissed me hard and slow. Surely, she is still behind the line in her black chef's hat and untied sneakers, making me grilled tofu with thick pats of butter. Where is she? I glimpse her shadow turning the corner, hear her bracelets twinkling faintly.

But of course, signs of change are here, too. The house where we used to live has shrunk. The cars in the driveway are all wrong. The yard is narrower than before, and the vast pond out back just a silver hand mirror now. The waitresses are younger than ever, and the church with the giant spire must have hiked up her skirt and walked three blocks west because surely that's not where she was before.

That night, we eat dinner in a seafood joint that somehow materialized inside the Bank of America. Afterward, we walk through town in the falling dusk, maneuvering through crowds on the sidewalk. The air tastes like chocolate, while ahead of us a man carries a slip of a girl maybe two years old on his shoulders. They wait at an intersection for the light to turn green. Two glittering gold studs in her earlobes catch the reflection of the red light.

She is dressed in a white and blue sailor suit; the cuffs of her white socks have frills that graze her father's stubbly cheeks. The child turns and finds me there in one swift motion.

Believe me when I say that our brown eyes lock and we are born back.

How else to describe it? The child and I—in that between space between light and dark, past and present—fall through a crack in the space-time continuum. We know one another. It is a moment of uncanny recognition. For that one interminable moment it is as if we are a single body outside time and space. Jack holds my hand, oblivious, and pulls us left at the intersection, but as we begin to move away, the child opens her eyes wide in terror and reaches for me in a panic. "Mama!" she cries. "Mama!"

* * * * *

In May, I am in the mountains of Vermont to teach at a four-day writing conference for high school students. They are hungry for validation, so I feed it to them in fistfuls. Here, alongside other members of this tribe of weirdos and book nerds, they feel real for maybe the first time. I want to hug them, show them glimpses of a future beyond the stultifying halls of high school, tell them it gets better. My phone rings right before a faculty meeting, as everyone is still milling around and making small talk. Jessie. "I'll call you back," I tell her. "I'm in a meeting and we're just about to go around the room and talk about how great we are. This is my favorite part."

She's silent on the other end, and then I hear sobbing, and I know instantly that she's lost the baby, which is a shitty euphemism but still the first words that come to mind, followed by a thud of *no*. "No," I say. "No, no, no." And then I flee the library clutching my phone.

When we were kids, Jessie lost everything. Keys, backpacks, wallets, purses. *Anything not nailed down*, her mother used to say. I cannot now calculate the hours we spent searching for her missing belongings, but it was one of the primary pastimes of our adolescence. Just as well, since we had nothing else to do. Boredom was the signature cocktail of our days. She was so wretched with loss, we started to believe in spirits, and blamed them for stealing and then furtively replacing her things. When we found the keys, or wallet, or purse, they were usually exactly where she had left them, where we had been looking all along. But a child is not a thing, she hasn't misplaced it, and there is no mischievous spirit cackling in the eaves—no deity that might render an empty body whole.

I kneel on the lawn beside the white clapboard library and cry. There is nothing I can say to comfort her, no balm or penance I might offer to undo what has always been coming. I close my eyes and will that I might materialize beside her in the bed—where I know without asking she is curled under the blankets—and hold her tight through the days and nights and weeks and years, if need be, until what she has lost is returned.

Chromosome 18, Monosomy 18P is a chromosomal disorder in which part of the short arm of chromosome 18 is truncated or deleted altogether. The doctor ordered a second ultrasound after technicians could not locate the nose bone. *Nothing to worry about*, they told Jessie. *The baby's probably just turned away from us. Common*, they said. *Just in case.*

Over speakerphone, a man they had never met before delivered the news. The fetus had a cleft lip and no facial bones. The brain had failed to divide into separate hemispheres. *Not sustainable*, he said. *A fluke*, he said. *Just one of those things.*

For four more days and nights, she had to carry the unsustainable fetus inside her. By the time my plane touched down in

Philadelphia, they had set a date for the abortion. Insurance would not cover the procedure, as it was considered an elective abortion. Weeks later, they mailed Jessie and Jon the paperwork. *Fetus*, it said. *20 weeks. Failure to thrive. Male.*

* * * * *

In August we return to Maine for the second year in a row: Jack and me, Hannah and Greg, Rya and Kara, and our friend Aryn. We stay in a 1920s cottage on the rocky shore of South Thomaston, owned by Greg's family friends. Rya is five months pregnant now, a summer squash, round and warm. I take her picture while she showers underneath the outdoor spigot, a stripe of sunlight down the left side of her body, her hands in her wet hair and her face to the sky. It's a beautiful photo. She looks healthy, full, and calm. For four days we swim in the frigid ocean, cook elaborate dinners, and ride our bikes along the coastal roadway to the lobster shack for lunch.

One hazy morning, Kara, Rya, and I kayak to a tiny, nearby island, deserted except for a single cabin. We peek through the windows and find it empty except for some books and an unmade bed, then climb the rocks along the shore. Kara has a beer tucked into her shorts like a pistol and we take turns peeing in the sand. I fantasize about living on an island like this one, starting from scratch, remaking the rules. Not an Island of Loss, but of Wonder—a place of impossible contradictions, lush and yet abandoned. I remember the book I'd read by the photographer Sally Mann, and how she'd named death a feminine energy—we are born of this energy and we eventually return to it. One night a few weeks before we came on this trip, while Jack was away visiting his parents in Maine, I went out into our backyard, built a fire in the firepit, and silently sang a siren song to the generations of women whose spirits were shattered, tossed out the backdoor, and folded into the land—not knowing how soon pieces of me, too, would be cast out alongside them.

Across the channel I make out our rented cottage next to a stand of pine trees, and our friends stretched out on bright beach towels on the front lawn, reading and talking. I see Jack with his giant camera draped around his neck taking pictures along the coastline. From this distance on my private island, I am overcome with love. I follow the mothers-to-be over pine needles, pebbles, and dusty sand. A dead snake hangs from a tree branch. A sneaker is half-covered in brush. As we paddle back to the small beach in front of the cottage, Jack crouches like the paparazzi, clicking and clicking. Next year, we'll have little Maven with us. I try to imagine those photos, and the changes they'll reveal in our faces. Whose sheen will be sallow? Whose eyes dark with grief? Whose hair gone wild? Which one of us will be missing?

*   *   *   *   *

Something else happened that night in Asheville. After the traffic light turned green and the father stepped out into the road, carrying the little girl aloft, and she screamed for me, her little hand flailing—*Mama! Maaaama!*—my brain emptied and my blood drained. I gasped and doubled over. Whatever doorway had opened just as quickly slammed shut. Despite myself, I buckled. Jack caught me before I fell to the sidewalk. I looked back for the child, but even as I heard her call to me she was already gone, the real world a wave that violently bore her away.

But this is the part I remember most vividly. Later, in bed, Jack was incredulous. "You imagined it," he said, turning on his laptop. "Anyway, I didn't see a kid," he said. He looked at me quickly and then away, and in that instant, I knew that he had.

*   *   *   *   *

The results are in. There is nothing genetically askew with their DNA and so Jessie and Jon start trying to get pregnant again. We don't talk about it. I don't ask her questions about how she feels or what it's like. I'm afraid that by asking she might shatter, and it will be a while before I realize how wrong I am. Years later, she'll tell me about her anger and pain, about the many hours she spent in the garden pulling weeds and weeping, and she'll tell me I got it wrong too. That she was not happy about having to carry her nonviable pregnancy for three days before she was able to terminate, but later she was grateful. It gave her time alone to process the loss, to wrap her arms around her belly and hold space for what remained of their time together. Why did I assume she would be livid at the doctors for making her wait? It was a failure of imagination, to not grant her this grace. Because all I felt was rage on her behalf, and to someone responsible for her pain. The doctors who made her wait were an easy target, but how minimizing it was to project my emotions onto her. It was her loss, not mine. And she had far more capacity to integrate it into her self-narrative than I had given her credit for.

What trick of evolution renders us alone in our losses? Surrounded, hopefully. Comforted, maybe. But ultimately alone. In our tumultuous twenties, my friends and I had formed a club out of a shared sense of loss and false pride for believing we'd left those losses behind, but what we shared was only the idea of grief and none of its jagged particularities. Jane is not Jonathan is not a body emptied is not a terror-induced incontinence is not a dead wife is not a protracted coming-out is not your bone-dry loneliness is not the persistent memory of a twin sister's caramelized breathing inside a coral pink hotel room along the steaming marshes of Disney World. We cannot divest ourselves of the ghosts of our own divining. All we can do is ask someone to look.

[LOVE & OTHER
LANGUAGE PROBLEMS]

Note: Italicized sections were written by my brother, Eric, during the winter of 2016, while serving a seventeen-month jail sentence in Philadelphia for attempted robbery. In the spring of 2017, he mailed me these meditations—six handwritten pages on yellow legal pad paper. I excerpt them here verbatim. Nonitalicized text is mine.

Sitting beside the woodstove, the windows letting in blue, winter light. After the wedding, the honeymoon in Spain, and now here, a house in Vermont for which Jack and I saved and scoured the tricounty area for a year. It feels like a momentous achievement, as if we'd built it ourselves, stone by stone. As if my whole life was in pursuit of this particular Saturday afternoon, this corner of Vermont, reading in a house I own while my husband brings in more wood from the woodpile, and the smell of snow and burning leaves follows him inside.

How deceptive such stories can be.

You're still in jail, will be for god knows how long and yes, this is a comfort. At least in jail you are safer from yourself, less likely to overdose, though I know you still manage to get high. You get a thrill out of telling me about it, the clever ways you sneak it in, like the guy's girlfriend who pushes a plastic coffee stirrer filled with crushed-up Oxy into his mouth with her tongue when they're kissing goodbye. I admit it's clever.

As I read, Jack hauls in another stack of logs for the woodstove. Clumps of snow fall from the giant fronds of a mulberry tree outside my window. Secreted inside the branches is a trilling chickadee. You couldn't stand the cold. Your fingers would freeze when you went out to smoke. My breath catches in my throat. I fall on my ass nearly every day on the icy front steps. These are trifling complaints to you, I know, but let's not compare our suffering.

The previous owners grew decadent gardens, and in the spring when they break soil it's like fresh blood blooming from a corpse. I have no idea how to tend a garden, you won't be surprised to hear. Did Mom keep even a single houseplant when we were growing up? Jack bought me a gardening book that I leave on the coffee table to impress guests. What I feel for the garden is a layman's love. I'll pull weeds, water it occasionally, and watch it giddily. I figure it is enough to look like a dedicated gardener. I don't have to be one too.

You asked about the sound in the background during our last call, prepaid minutes ticking away, an automated voice reminding us, "ten minutes remaining." I was sitting outside for a few brief minutes in late afternoon, my face to the pale sun, trying to absorb whatever heat she deigned to throw my way. Chickadees rummaged the bushes for scraps, still trilling loudly.

"Um, birds?" I said. "You remember birds, don't you? How long have you been locked up?"

Right, birds.

We laughed, and I remembered suddenly the time when I was seven and you were five and we'd wept over a cardinal that had flown headlong into our grandparent's kitchen window and then lay heaving on the hot slate patio, one eyeball dangling limply from its socket.

"Actually, there was a bird in the showers the other day," you said. "But then it flew into a window and died."

Right, birds.

You'll be in there for at least another year, your thirty-fourth revolution around this tempestuous sun. You were on probation when you relapsed, and then you robbed a guy, or tried to anyway. Of course, the story doesn't make sense. You followed him as he exited the bus somewhere in Northeast Philly. You told him you had a gun, but you did not have a gun. Something squirreled under your T-shirt, maybe, meant to look like a gun. But even claiming to have a gun changes the nature of the charges. The man "feared for his life."

Well, don't we all?

I picture mist and shuffling and the striking, silver edge of the heroin leaving your system. Something cold and razor-sharp beneath the skin. A primal sadness. I cannot picture you with a gun, only as a big-eared boy-child crying, crying, always crying, lips fat and glistening wet.

Once, you explained that the goal is to "fish out," meaning to come so close to death that you flop around like a hooked bass. But then you don't die. By some impossible grace, you are released into black waters and you don't die.

I imagine you thought briefly, dumbly: *Fuck this guy. I will fuck him up. All smug and shit. What's he got that I don't?* You told the cop that the guy had stolen a woman's wallet on the bus, and you—hero of a thousand myths—had only been trying to get it back for her.

It reminds me of that old AA joke about the difference between an alcoholic and a drug addict. *An alcoholic will steal your wallet, but a drug addict will steal your wallet and then help you look for it.* It's the kind of joke that makes you say, "That's funny," instead of actually laughing. When the cop pinned you to the sidewalk and turned your pockets inside out there was no gun, no money, no cell phone even, just the man's used-up bus pass.

Do you remember the day you and Mom dropped me off at college in New Hampshire? How, after the two of you left, you only made it thirty miles before you burst into tears? You, sixteen, skinny, cocky man-boy. High half the time. "Go get her," you cried to Mom. "We have to go back and get her!" Mom told me this story later. I think she thought it would make me feel good to know how much you needed me.

What it made me feel, though, is that I'd fucked up. That I was selfish. I can admit this to you now. I knew you needed me and I left anyway. That's what I felt then. I wonder now if a small part of Mom intended the story to induce this guilt. It's true that the three of us were interdependent then. We were complicit in one another's unhealthy coping mechanisms. Mom was doing bong rips in the basement with us. She brought us toast and coaxed us to swallow. You were stoned all the time. I was doing Ritalin and starving myself. Staying would not have killed me, but a self-preservation instinct kicked in and I fled the first chance I got. I thought you'd make it out too. I believed it until I couldn't anymore.

∗　∗　∗　∗　∗

[Eric]: *Mom always gets the story wrong. You should know that by now. You wanna know the real story?*

You do but you don't.

I'm standing in a nasty, dark, dingy alley in the Badlands section of Philadelphia. There are used needles, used cookers, chip wrappers, Honey Bun wrappers, and chunks of gravel and concrete. The alley itself is long and narrow and I'm standing about five feet in from the opening to the street. I'm leaning on an eight-foot-high wooden fence, on the other side of which is a yard full of old and broken kids' toys, a few flat tires with rusted rims, and what looks like a brand new dirt bike.

I look up at the moon and take a deep breath, watching it disappear into the chilly night as I exhale.

Every five minutes or so I hear a car drive by on Fifth Street, but other than that no noise. No noise until I hear the unmistakable "click-clack" of someone racking the slide on a pistol, pulling a bullet into the chamber. A second later that pistol is pressed to the side of my head. I'd just robbed the dude for sixty bucks while he was getting his dick sucked by some hooker. The hooker and I had planned it earlier in the night.

I'm standing there waiting to buy some coke, having injected a little more than an eight-ball throughout the latter part of the day and earlier tonight, and I'm crashing hard and really need a pick-me-up. I scrounge up my last sixty dollars, money that was supposed to go toward transportation to meet my girl who was just released from jail earlier today. I stop first at my usual block, but they are in for the night due to an earlier raid. I call an old number and hope for the best.

*   *   *   *   *

When dad died when we were teenagers—drunk and headlong down that flight of stairs—I absorbed his love into the wound of my body. It sounds crazy, but I swear I felt it. His love was a bottomless pit of wanting. Jack had been right, all those years ago, when he told me I wanted to fuck the whole world. I didn't want to die, I just wanted to dissolve into light. Maybe you understand.

Dad's death was a wonder. There was a man and then there wasn't. He wore flannel shirts and work boots and his breath smelled like spearmint gum and cigarettes and we were on our way to visit him, you and me, but he was not there to be visited. He was dead, but we knew he was alive. In the car, we had the carton of Camel Lights he had asked for. I wore his old T-shirt. We were going to eat spaghetti and listen to Bonnie Raitt. This was a fact, but it was not a fact because he was dead. We did not know it then, in the car, on the way to visit him. He was already dead. He had fallen through the sky, drunk under the undressing moon, and he was dead, dead, dead, amen.

* * * * *

[Eric]: *Then there is a cocked and loaded pistol pressed to the side of my head. I slowly turn so I am facing the guy, noticing his scuffed Timberland boots, black Nike sweatpants, black Nike hoodie, and a black Carhart skully. It's odd the things we notice under stress, because only now do I focus on the gun, which is pointed between my eyes. When I turn, he takes a step back, which makes me think that he has held a gun to someone before; if he remained too close, I could have grabbed it.*

I don't want to try to portray myself as a tough guy who has guns put to his head regularly, but still lives to tell about it, because I'm not. I'm a strung-out cokehead, down to his last sixty dollars, which makes me many things—but two things in particular—desperate and dangerous. Desperate because I need a fix, and dangerous to myself or anyone who stands in my way. Also, at this point in my life, I am extremely depressed and apathetic, a treacherous combination. When a man is pointing a loaded nine-millimeter at your head, but you look in his eyes with a "I don't give a fuck how this goes" look, it unnerves him a little. I also don't think he is overly surprised when he tells me to give him the money and I flat-out tell him no. I make a fist around those three greasy, sweaty twenty-dollar bills and say, "The only way you're getting this money is by shooting me, so go ahead and catch a body over sixty dollars, you fucking idiot."

* * * * *

Mom gets confused sometimes and says things to me like, "Remember when we were raising Eric?" Usually she corrects herself, but sometimes she doesn't and waits for an earnest answer, dripping cigarette ash on her pants. But the thing is, as your surrogate father, I was a disgrace. What kind of father mocks and demeans their kid? Beats him up for stealing their Biggie Smalls CD? Ignores him for weeks, never plays catch, can't fix a toaster or help a kid navigate puberty? I did not teach you how to talk about your feelings, or interview for a job, or save your money. I couldn't mirror back to you your own best self, model manhood, or even pick it out in a lineup. Once, I kicked you in the balls for turning off MTV. Once, I made you give me all your Ritalin so my friends and I could snort it over the weekend. Once, I laughed in your face while you cried. More than once.

"We should have sent him to Boy Scout camp," I say.
"Montessori was a bad idea," she says.

Here's what I know now: I had no business trying to parent you. I was a child myself, and we were navigating all the same losses. And still when I read your letters, I can't help but feel responsible for your pain. I left for college. I chose to save myself. I do not regret it.

One of our new neighbors is in a wheelchair. He either had an accident or was born with a congenital condition. Every day, he wails from his porch. A deep, guttural wail. I hear it all day long. Sometimes, I imagine that if death were a sound, that would be it. This agonizing cry. Then I imagine having a baby beside me, and how her cries would be the opposite of his cries. Cries of hunger, yearning, life. Cries I could quell with my body. My purview.

———

[LOVE & OTHER LANGUAGE PROBLEMS]

158

My therapist says it's self-aggrandizing to think I have any control over your fate. I have to stop trying to figure it out. There's nothing I can do, she says, and so I quit.

One black night last January during one of your worst binges, after years of rehabs and relapses and too many overdoses, Mom and I were exhausted. We sat smoking on her back porch as usual. Waiting for a phone call. A yes or no. Alive or dead. This future or that one.

"Would it be better?" I whispered.

"If he died?"

"Yeah."

She took three long drags before answering.

"Maybe," she said.

She didn't look at me then or for the rest of the night. She went inside and up to bed.

* * * * *

I knew when I'd had my first proper orgasm because it felt like dying. In French, in modern usage, *la petite mort* refers specifically to "the sensation of post-orgasm as likened to death." It can refer to the spiritual release that comes with orgasm or to "a short period of melancholy or transcendence as a result of the expenditure of the 'life force.'"

It took me twenty-nine years, but after my first real orgasm I realized that perhaps the "life instinct" and the "death instinct" are the same instinct. Maybe we spend our whole lives resisting death, not realizing that it's what we're here to achieve. The salmon that run in the river near my new home know this; they spawn then die. Praying mantises do it better: the female bites off the head of the male while mating, then devours his corpse for nourishment. Roland Barthes spoke of *la petite mort* as the signature experience of reading great literature.

Consider wonder. I found in the *Oxford English Dictionary* a shared connection between "wonder" and "wounding" in the entry's "obsolete" listings. These listings define "wonder" as variously "omen or portent," "an evil or shameful action," "evil or horrible deeds," "destruction, disaster," or "great distress or grief." So, what we might think of as purely good, as Socrates explained wonder, contains good and evil. Joy and pain. Life and death. Furthermore, I learn, we experience wonder most frequently when the familiar goes suddenly strange. A child encountering the ocean for the first time. Your hands no longer looking like your hands. Jesus speaking through the television set. The child you were always meant to have failing to manifest. Your lover's face when he no longer loves you.

Your mother's body divested of a piece of itself, a lung, say, which she had used her whole life to smoke.

It's getting late. Jack is making dinner. I won't tell you what he's making; it'll only make you jealous (lasagna). Dear god, the snow. It's windy and freezing. I keep smelling must rising from the floorboards. Sometimes, I think this house is full of ghosts. Maybe anticipatory grief makes it easier to understand the wound in wonder, but it also means I am never truly alone in it. The world is full of such anticipations.

*   *   *   *   *

[Eric]: *I'd like to say the reason I told him to pull the trigger was because I was tough and brave, calling this pussy's bluff before I took his* gun from him and beat him with it. That was not the case. The real reason I said those words to him was because I was such a coward, running from my demons, and I knew by saying what I said it would end in one of two ways.

The first ending would be a bullet in my head, immediately and permanently ending my self-inflicted hell. In the second ending, he would be so thrown off-balance by my utter disregard for my own life over sixty dollars—and not wanting to end a life over such a trivial amount—that he lets me walk out of there, money in hand, thus enabling me to buy the drugs I'd originally sought out as a temporary solution to the pain.

Ultimately, he ended up violently shoving me toward the opening of the alley, yelling, "Get the fuck outta here."

At the time, I remember being angry that I didn't get the permanent solution. My mother's pain getting a phone call from a Philadelphia homicide detective to come ID her only son's body? Fuck it. Who cares about her? At least I am not in pain anymore, right? My sister trying to find the strength to help organize her little brother's closed-casket funeral, dealing with her own grief, trying to find a way to take her next breath while simultaneously trying to be a pillar for my mother to lean on? Well, at least I don't have to think about that; I'm gone.

Fuck them. Isn't that what I'm saying walking around with a death wish? Fuck them.

I run over to the car my friend was waiting in and jump in. I tell him what happened and direct him to a different block so we can buy what we need. I was supposed to have picked up my girlfriend from Delaware County Jail at noon. It's going to be midnight by the time I make it up there.

Priorities, right?

* * * * *

It's the day after the election. Yesterday, when I first found out the results, I didn't think I would make it to class. Thirty-seven undergraduates were waiting for me to say something comforting, something smart. I sat on the porch in the freezing cold and cried. Jack came outside and put his hand on my shoulder. His car was warming up. I stared at the exhaust fumes and didn't know what to say. I still don't. What he said next, though, recapitulated everything I thought I knew about him. "Give him a chance," he said. *Give him a chance?* He heard the man talking about grabbing pussies, right? About Mexicans being thugs? About endless dangerous, bombastic, vile bullshit? I watched him walk away through the snow in his leather L.L. Bean boots and amorphous, middle-class ennui. Had he posted that comment on social media I would have been baffled, but when he said it out loud, *to his wife*, I heard something more sinister: a man who believes he can't lose. I don't imagine you feel this way. You've already lost everything a man can lose. It doesn't make you morally superior, just keenly aware of how capitalist systems deal with deviation. Which is to say, mercilessly.

What I really want to know, though, is if you ever let yourself imagine something different.

I went to class. I didn't know what else to do. I thought I should be there for my students even if I couldn't offer them anything particularly encouraging. Theirs is not a passive grief. The internet has empowered them. They are not afraid to say who they are and how they feel. Ten years ago, when I first started teaching college, this was not the case. My students were still in the closet, still quietly ashamed of themselves, still deferential to power. They called me "Dr. Nelson" even though I don't have a PhD and thanked me after every class. I did not correct them about the PhD.

This semester I'm teaching personal essay, so we tell the stories we think make a kind of sense of the chaos of the moment. We order and reorder these stories, amend, and double back. We're all looking for truer shapes for our lives. At eighteen, they've already developed habits and healthy suspicions. Their stories are slippery and poorly structured. They get frustrated. The stories they submit can't be filtered with vintage gold or validated by likes. One student wrote about her recent DUI arrest and her father's subsequent disavowals. Another, a trans man, wrote about his double mastectomy and the tender way his three-year-old niece traced his scars in the pool last summer while the rest of his family looked on, gnawing on chicken wings and whispering. The more complicated the story, the less it's valued by the internet. I want to explain this to them but with what feeble authority? A woman with so much longing and so few followers?

Sometimes they write funny things in their end-of-semester evaluations, like *Dr. Nelson is really enthusiastic, but she has no time management skills.* Or *Dr. Nelson is often frazzled and chugging coffee even though our class is at four in the afternoon.*

If they only knew.

Sometimes they blink at me like mice. They're looking for step-by-step instructions, but there's no manual. They think writing is something that can be tackled linearly, like building an IKEA desk or baking a cake. Sometimes, when they come to my office crying, I feel a maternal urge to hug them. Imagine what they'd write in the evaluations if I did.

* * * * *

[Eric]: *"Local response to H-2! Local response to H-2!" the voice booms over the intercom. It's routine at this point, it means there's a fight on that particular block and any CO nearby needs to drop everything and run there. The CO left on our block has us clear the dayroom and crowds everyone onto the lower tier. I'm lying in my bunk reading and doing my best to ignore this inconvenience. I hear the squeaking of sneakers* like you might hear on a basketball court when a player plants his foot. It's a sound I'm familiar with and right away I know that two people on my block are fighting pretty much right outside my door. I don't bother to get up and look because it's always over by the time I get there. My celly, however, moves to the window and tells me what he sees. He describes a bigger dark-skinned guy with another guy in a headlock, simultaneously swinging a sharp homemade knife into the other guy's head and neck. It's taking a long time for anyone to respond and the bigger guy continues stabbing over and over. After they separate, the guy who was getting stabbed stumbles past my door dazed and bloody. One gash on the back of his neck, in particular, looks pretty bad, cut to the white meat. This event unfortunately is just as common as the fistfight going on in the other block.

Just another day in PICC. I've become so accustomed to it that I don't even worry if the guy's ok or not. I don't stop and stare. I just go back to reading my book, brooding over the fact that my visiting hours will be canceled and the block will be locked down for a few days. They need to shake down a couple times now looking for the weapon. They bring dogs on the block every morning, sniffing for blood and drugs. They cut off the phones and showers. All routine. All mundane. All a part of my everyday life now. Everyday life here includes showering with boxers on and sandals on your feet. It's wearing sneakers at all times as opposed to sandals because you never know when you need to fight or defend yourself. It's turning around so your back is against the wall while you're on the phone so you can see what and where everyone is at all times. It's not using the Papi phone without permission or the Muslim phone without permission. It's knowing where to hide your contraband, when to smoke, how to approach a cell or enter one. It's knowing without being taught. It's a 24/7 lesson in survival. It's what I've learned years ago through different jails and ruthless streets. It's a whole different me that I turn on when I'm here, and off when I'm on the phone with the outside world. It's someone my family need not know exist. They see their son or little brother. The one who cried nonstop for years growing up, the one who always ran to Mom to help pick up the pieces. The sensitive, caring, kind, intelligent, and funny Eric. They don't know that out of necessity,

I've built a switch, one I can turn on in the blink of an eye. My survival switch. Put me in North Philly, Kensington, Las Vegas, juvenile lockups and maximum-security prisons, I can survive. I don't always like the person, but I make it through. It's not to say I lose who I am either. I still have a sense of humor; I'll always care about other people. It's little additions, it's a heightened awareness of my surroundings and environment. It's been my life for a while now. My mother always asks me, what's next? What will you do when you're released from jail, rehab, halfway house, recovery house?

I don't know. Does it really matter? Because just surviving from day to day have I ever accomplished anything? Have I put in any type of significant work or effort toward a meaningful soul? Have I even taken just one step forward? Anything positive at all? Anyone? Hello?

No.

No matter how many times I've picked the pieces up, no matter what I've tried—AA, NA, Methadone, Suboxone, recovery houses, halfway houses, in the city, out of the city—it doesn't matter. Two months clean or nine months clean. Drug of choice heroin, coke, crack, Xanax, or Percocet. None of it matters.

But I survive. Which means I can.

*　*　*　*　*

Socrates claims that all philosophy begins in wonder: *thaumazein* in Greek. *Thaumazein* is an irresolvable contradiction—in the way that a child is both of his parents and entirely his own being—and to be lost in wonder, he says, means you're on the track toward wisdom. In fact, in Socratic philosophy, this notknowing is the height of human wisdom, a moment of realization when something that was once self-evident proves false. *You survive, which means you can.* Except if you don't. The best stories (mine, yours) are rooted in wonder. They ask the reader to accept contradictory truths in the same breath. I know having a kid would not be an answer to my question: *What can I make out of this one temporal body to warrant the life that you do not get to live?*

Instead, I write about you. We are more intimate in these pages than we've ever been in life.

Once upon a time, your mother dreamed you alive. You were the last of her creative imperatives. Now, she is not well. She is racked with worry. Her body is bloated and weak, loose-limbed and slow. Belly full of wine. She smokes and coughs, smokes and coughs. Her body wakes her up in the middle of the night to smoke. I smell it seeping under the door to the guest room when I visit. It is more than she can take. I know, because once we shared a body and now we share this grief. When she asks me, again and again, when I'm getting pregnant, I can't help but think maybe it would be the impetus for her to quit. But then I remember you, and how nothing we ever did or said changed the course of your addiction. Then I remember you, and I freeze.

While I wait to hear if you are dead or alive, I make dinner and think about the garden. Some nights, I drink kinda good wine and sleep in a bed big as an ocean liner. I worry the garden will die; that Trump will get us into a nuclear war with North Korea; that my dumb, waning fertility will beat itself out inside of me.

Eric, here's the truth: it took me longer than it should have to realize you were writing these letters for an imagined audience larger than just me. A friend pointed it out. *Oh, god,* she said, rolling her eyes, *he's the tragic hero of his own devising!* How manipulative. I was indignant. *Oh, god,* I said. Except hadn't I spent the last decade mining your life for the scraps of my stories? Why wouldn't you want some of that agency back? To write yourself into power? I recalled all the times you'd asked me to ghostwrite your story, turn it into a memoir with your name on it—as if you could skip the decades of training, practice, rejections, the spit and grunt and white-knuckled labor of becoming a writer. As if you could simply dash off some letters only to have them appear, wholesale, inside the pages of a published book. I've done the work, and love is a language problem I still can't solve. I tried, *oh, god*, how I tried. So here are your letters. Your adoring audience. Here is your story back. Take it and go.

[LA PETITE MORT]

After the wood has been stacked and the dishes washed, Jack and I take to our new bedroom. I spread for him, a plume of flesh. He puts his mouth on me and I grab his hair and pull him closer. I want to fit his whole body inside of me. He flips me over and fucks me from behind while I watch the bare branches of our oak trees list inside the fog. While he is inside me, I am not lonely. I am not afraid. We sway with the trees and form a cosmology. It is him, me, the trees, the swaying. We are our whole world. He comes inside the condom, and it feels like a small violence not to have him fill me up. When I come, I feel a deep desolation—a chasm of sorrow. I cry. Not the soft, coquettish tears of pleasure and joy, but the deepest, ugliest bleating of worst grief. I don't know where it comes from or where it goes when it leaves my body.

"Yes," Jack says. "Yes, it's okay." He rubs my chest and says he likes it when I cry.

But it feels like dying, I want to say.

He says, "That's how I know it was good."

[RUNNING IN PLACE]

The trailhead is across the street from the liquor store in Winooski, Vermont, the town where I used to live. I say I am running, but really I am walking and occasionally lifting my feet a little faster, mostly where the trail slopes downward and gravity takes hold, into a cadence that might be perceived—by an eager dog, say—as something resembling a jog. The day is bright and lucid. It is late September, a ticking of days before Jack will leave me without warning, and here in Vermont the leaves are burning orange and red. At least, those that haven't been sold on the internet and shipped to places like Albuquerque and San Bernardino in vacuum-sealed zip-locked baggies for twenty dollars a dozen. The Vermont Leaf Company it's called, two guys in their early sixties, one tall and ponytailed who speaks with a German accent. I saw them on the news. The other guy, Frank, is short, round, with thinning hair dyed a dark red-brown. His accent sounds more like New Jersey, or Poughkeepsie maybe.

There is a Vermont [——] Company for just about anything Vermonters can produce or pilfer: cheese, maple syrup, tea, coffee, flannel, wine, craft beer, ice, teddy bears. Not to mention Ben and Jerry's. Sometimes, Vermont feels less like a real place, and more like a vision in the collective consumer imagination. It's an idealized image of life; a Pinterest portrait of mindful living; a set of aesthetics masquerading as ethics. This local, organic, vegan, paleo, hand-churned, free-range, artisanal, micro-batch potato chip is not just a snack, but evidence of our moral superiority. But only if you 'gram it.

What I've learned from living in Vermont for the last seven years is that you can't ever be Vermonty enough for Vermont. You can always Vermont better: eat, act, and live more Vermontly. Your friends are either "makers" or you make other friends. Your child's diapers are not cloth enough; your beer never sufficiently local; your politics, no matter where they land, are neither progressive nor conservative enough. Vermont, for all her beauty, steals your identity and then sells the improved version back to you for double the price.

I am not immune to the allure of tribalism, nor its financial dividends. If I were to start a company in Vermont it would be the Vermont Jewish Deli company and it would be wildly popular and make me rich. Vermonters would line up around the block, bring my bagels to the swap meet and smile smugly, post pictures of my nova glowing pink and ethereal as baby Jesus cheeks. But I don't open the Vermont Jewish Deli company, despite knowing it would be wildly popular and make me rich, because I am vain and afraid of failure. Also, because Vermont is not known for Jewish delis, or Jewish anything really save Bernie, and maybe it would confuse people and not make me rich after all. Maybe I would lose my shirt and wind up half-naked and smelling like gefilte fish, hocking jars of hand-cured salmon on the internet to mitigate my losses. Made in Vermont.

"We're also known for foliage," said Frank in the news segment yesterday, "and nobody's shipping Vermont leaves? I had to jump on that."

Bear in mind, Frank's website warns, *leaves decompose over time.*

The website features stock images of Vermont scenery—so many red clapboard barns framed by towering maples, a lone cow grazing in the foreground—as well as a helpful album of Pinterest craft ideas: *Why not trace an intricate mountain horizon on your leaf, then cut it out with a razor blade?* I imagine decomposing leaf-art tucked inside sun-warmed windowsills, their pretty cut-out images shriveling to dust, beyond which a desert cactus blooms. The leaf dust collects on a white windowsill where it remains for months before somebody decides to sweep it into her palm. She might then pluck the delicately ribbed leaf skeleton from its perch beside the window lock. Curling it into her fist, the ribs crackle and break, dust now too, and are brushed into the trash can. Outside, the desert cactus is so still, conceding to the moon. What does our leaf artist do then? Does she go outside in the moonlight? Does she return to the website to order more? So much bounty right here at my feet, and not a single cactus bloom.

* * * * *

When we were younger, my brother and I stole our father's tape collection—Bonnie Raitt, Indigo Girls, Genesis, Led Zeppelin— and sold them door to door for a dollar apiece. We picked our neighbors' flowers and made bouquets wrapped in tinfoil that we sold on the next street over. Eric is a natural salesman, like most members of my mother's side of the family. I remember clearly the day he toddled up to our neighbor's door and sold her back her own flowers, with the upcharge for the extra daffodil.

"I'm not selling leaves to *Vermonters!*" Frank says, looking straight into the camera.

Frank is *fearless*, the newscasters want us to understand. There are people who see an opportunity and jump on it. I'm not sure what separates those who jump from those who don't, but I suspect it has to do with imagination. Imagination is what separates humans from other life forms, scientists say, the ability to imagine a distant future and plan for it. We envision a future and make practical steps toward making it a reality, they say. Frank imagined a life in which he spent his days foraging for colorful *leaves*, packing them into *Ziploc baggies*, and carting his bounty to the *post office*, where it would then be whisked away to faraway doorsteps. In exchange, people would give Frank *money*. They would not be upset when their purchases shriveled and decomposed, because he would warn them straight away, *right on the website!*

Scientists don't say anything about a future that presents itself without warning. Or why we can imagine certain futures and not the ones that end up befalling us, despite our best efforts.

I miss Winooski, so I make excuses to come back. Today, I've just finished teaching a class and made this pit stop for a quick run before driving the thirty miles south to our new home. I don't yet know how brief my time will be in Waterbury, Vermont, home of Ben & Jerry's, the only recently shuttered Vermont State Hospital (a.k.a. Vermont Insane Asylum), and not much else. Before we bought our house in Waterbury we lived here in Winooski for four years, a tiny town adjacent to Burlington, the state's largest "city" with a population of roughly forty thousand. Winooski is often referred to as the "Brooklyn of Burlington," but is little more than a single traffic circle containing a few restaurants, bars, shops, a nearby YMCA, the VFW, Shaw's Grocery Store, and one square mile of residential homes and apartments along the Winooski River. My friend at the gas station recently told me that Winooski means "onion" in Abenaki, the language of the native tribe who used to live on this land, eating the wild onions that flourished along the riverbanks. Today, the population of Winooski is only about seven thousand, many of whom are Bhutanese, Nepalese, Somalian, and Bosnian refugees, in other words, the most diverse town in Vermont by a long stretch. Our recent move from Winooski to Waterbury, approximately thirty miles south and eight shades whiter, came with mixed feelings, and at times seems like yet another lurch-

ing descent into the white, middle-class, heteronormative ho-
mogeny to which I had never anticipated belonging so abso-
lutely. Yet, I confess I am wearing yoga pants. Though I do not
own a Subaru, I've caught myself fantasizing about keeping my
skis accessible in a hatchback all winter. *Cross-country* skis no
less. And I've been known to "juice," all of which is a far cry from
the way I was raised—Jewish, dysfunctional, and unkempt. My
mother is not so much disapproving as bemused. She will not,
under any circumstances, come with me to Jazzercise during
her visits. "What the fuck is a CSA?" she asks, dragging on her
cigarette. "You mean CSI," she decides.

Yet it will be some time before I admit to myself that I don't feel
home in Vermont anymore. I don't feel home in my marriage.
I don't feel home in my adjunct teaching "career." I don't feel
home in Vermont's inhospitable winters or even her brief but fe-
cund summers. But first, rather than admit it, I'd doubled down,
searching for a home to buy as frantically as if someone were
holding a gun to my head. *Invest your paltry adjunct income into
the faltering economy of a rapidly aging state or you're dead meat*, said
my imagined assassin. Later, I'll realize why—I was trying to put
into place circumstances in which Jack might change his mind
about us having kids. As if dressing in the accoutrement of family life magically creates one; empty bedrooms suddenly manifesting tiny occupants; a dining room table conjuring tiny, hungry tyrants into each of its chairs. For a whole year, I spent four to
six hours a day on Zillow, going on countless drive-bys because
Jack refused to go through "one more shitbox." I thought every
house had *potential*—contained an implicit, new, and newly solid
life for us. Suddenly and inexplicably, at age thirty-two and after over a decade of moving around willy-nilly, I needed desperately to stay put. Where once I had treasured the ability to pick
up and move whenever the mood struck, I now felt this peripa-
tetic lifestyle to be a liability. Time spooled out in front of me
like a severed ribbon. The boxing and unboxing of a life, the
constant breakdown and rebuilding, gobbled up precious mo-

ments I'd rather spend digging into the earth than skimming over it. Potential renovations were not projects but a plotting of days through which I could envision us moving in meticulous detail. Here was a way to harness time. Not the poured concrete countertops so much as the pouring of the concrete itself. Not the solid lumber of the back deck, but the seconds, minutes, and hours we would spend on that deck—drinking coffee and carrying out plates of steaming food for friends and family—food that we grow in our own garden, rooted in the slow circadian revolutions of earth time. Not the swell and dips of the lawn, but the mowing, mowing, mowing of it. Such tending, I suspected, would harness the white sheet of time, grab it by all four corners and pull time taut around us. Each house had its own set of needs and pleasures that anticipated and accounted for time. Indulging those fantasies felt like magic (I was *imagining!*); it felt like a superpower. So many potential futures scattered across the mountains and valleys of Vermont, and each one easily accessible via the internet; I needed only refresh the website, check again in five minutes. In one house, I am a mother. A naked girl-child roams the woods in the backyard. She picks her nose and watches too much TV and eats blueberries from the cluster of blueberry bushes by the garage. In another house, twins, a boy and a girl who I can only envision as infants tucked into the crib Jack has made out of pine and stained a dark walnut. In some houses, I am a reclusive but impossibly stylish writer, childless, traveling half the year. I wanted to try them all on, casting my future onto ever more blank living room walls. Bypassing anything felt like a violence. Each house possessed a long and living history into which I might simply plug in, lighting my body at both ends. I could manifest anything this way.

I became obsessed. I checked the Zillow app during a funeral. I canceled my classes on more than one occasion, only to drive past homes I knew definitively would not work for us—a dilapidated ranch two hours from where we worked; a three-thousand-square-foot Victorian without running water; a remodeled New

Englander with a gleaming black metal roof and fifty thousand dollars over budget. I attended open houses on the sly, slinking past sign-in sheets and returning with groceries to explain my absences. Over the course of a year, I dragged our realtor—a tiny, fashionable blonde woman in her midforties who we nicknamed Julie Zoom-Zoom—to more than sixty houses. She'd pull up in her slinky white sports car, smiling white teeth, and tromp beside us across mud-heavy yards and into damp nineteenth-century basements wearing six-inch stiletto heels and crisp linen pants, impossibly good-natured and patient. Settling down, I felt suddenly and urgently, meant settling in. It meant being still. As in "not moving," but also, we can't break up when we're in the middle of re-tiling the kitchen. Nobody dies in the middle of home maintenance, I thought.

Except I would find out soon how wrong that was.

I was trying to distract us both from the one truth we were still ignoring: I wanted a child and he didn't. If I dressed up that potentiality in cedar shingles and fertile garden beds, he'd see my vision. My little ghost.

* * * * *

A few summers ago, soon after Jack and I had moved to Winooski, a tractor trailer coming from Canada lost control during a storm and toppled over the bridge railing to land along the riverbank below, near to where I am now, still "running." In photos from the accident, the truck looks like a crumpled Tonka toy, something chewed up and spit out. It took weeks to remove the bulk of the wreckage, and months before the cab finally disappeared. It nestled jauntily between the trees like a grinning, decapitated head.

It was about this same time when I heard about the local man who had been caught harboring a preserved human brain in a jar beneath his front porch, which he had reportedly stolen from a lab somewhere, and from which he had been siphoning formaldehyde to boost the potency of his ditch weed. He'd named the brain Frank.

Car accidents are major news in Vermont, to say nothing of the occasional organ-napping, and a bad one can garner days of coverage. When we moved to Vermont from New York five years ago, this sort of small-town journalism freaked me out. I was accustomed to the news in Philadelphia, where I had grown up, and where the nightly lineup usually sounded like dispatches from a war zone: *murder, murder, rape, arson, murder, rape, murder, moment of silence.*

Top stories in Vermont, I learned quickly after moving here, often include coverage of various high school sports games and fishing derbies, debates over farming and parking regulations, and the simultaneously bemoaned and beloved Montreal tourists who come for the foliage and lower sales taxes, but don't tip well. And still, Vermont will seduce you. The morning of our Vermont barn wedding (in our defense, it was 2015), we'd ushered our guests to a nearby river for a swim. The water flowed around stones flat as pancakes and caught in little green eddies underneath cascading willow trees. A red-haired teenager, long and lean, came tromping by, crunching an apple he'd plucked from a nearby tree. As he casually tossed off his T-shirt, stooped to place the apple beside it, and dove into the cool blue river, Jessie's sister Ashley turned to me, mouth agape. "Is this fucking real life?" she whispered. "Is this a real place?"

* * * * *

I was born just outside of Philly and grew up in a lower-middle-class suburb called Ambler, which for three-quarters of a century was known as the "Asbestos-Making Capital of the World," and which today has been gentrified beyond recognition. For eighteen years my occasional trips into Philadelphia looked nothing like the news portrayals, which seemed to feature exclusively murders, fires, murders by arson, attempted murders, Eagles football, and murders committed by Eagles fans. But to a kid from "The Town Abstestos Built," Philly was a theme park, a disco, a slaphappy montage of cartoon characters and museum exhibits. Benjamin Franklin tuning his kite on the soft green at Washington Square Park; Betsy Ross smiling absently as she rocked, sewing the same stars onto the same American flag for years; the flamboyant chacachaca of South Street, colorful beaded curtains shimmering across storefront windows while men in calypso skirts slipped into cavernous, pulsing movie theaters that played *The Rocky Horror Picture Show* for weeks on end; the giant human heart in the Franklin Institute into which I would insert my whole self, a single red blood cell running through the ridges of stiff, plastic arteries, sliding down the superior vena cava to land at my mother's feet.

For a few years my father worked in asbestos removal. I remember the protective jumpsuit he shed every evening in the laundry room, white dust collecting on the floor that he'd then sweep into the yard. Only now, so many years later, does it occur to me that this practice probably nullified the protections of the suit. Had he not died from complications related to alcohol and drug addiction at forty-four, he would have been a strong candidate for mesothelioma—the same cancer the TV lawyers used to trumpet about on daytime commercials, their 1-800 numbers repeated ad nauseum.

Home is the site and source of our greatest wonder. Its magic and its miseries. It's where we first discover our sexuality and where we first explore it. And if we are lucky enough to receive love there, home is also where we learn how fickle that love can be. Our caretakers hold us, then shun us for waking up in the middle of the night. One day our bruises are tended, the next they are ignored. Home is where we meet our first ghosts, the ones under the bed and the glittery ones who bear us aloft in dreams. Sometimes we have parents who tell us sweet things and kiss our faces and read us books and then disappear forever. When I left Philadelphia for college in New Hampshire, life instantly improved. In my eighteen-year-old brain, I equated a change in environment with a change in quality of life. Each time I traveled somewhere new, or moved to a different state, those same signals fired. It was the newness that delighted me, and the chance to remake my life for the better. Moving forward in life became synonymous with changing my environment. But now we're here in Vermont and Jack never wants to move again. No matter my doubts—the weather, the small-town ethos—or my innate compulsion to try something new, making our home here is the logical next step. Rather than avoid it, I'd gone all in on this idea. I believed it was a kind of sanctuary. I would be safe inside a world of my own design. And yet, in moments, I cannot shake the dissonance I feel. My brother, my love, is the hatchet hanging over my head, threatening at any second to sever me from this glorious, tenuous, light-dappled hidey hole 383 miles north from where we were born and grew up, flailing bigheaded infants dropped into the deep end of the life pool, and where he remains, still in jail—donning a blue one-piece jumpsuit, balding, tall and thin, high-fiving again today his eighteen-year-old celly called Dutch—waiting for the hearing that never comes, the deal never brokered, the treatment never procured, the faceless public defender who never shows up.

And me? Planting tomatoes and feasting on expensive Vermont cheeses. *Oh, god.*

Vermont, a fertility I can't possibly deserve.

* * * * *

It is hard to muster pride for the Asbestos Capital of the World. Vermonters, however, are very proud of Vermont. They are proud of their cheese and beer and teddy bears and leaves and skiing and syrup and their farm-to-table everything. They are proud of their politics, though often ignore the fact that their politics vary widely depending, it seems, on one's proximity to the I-89 corridor. They are proud of their community-mindedness (there is more than one documentary about Waterbury's inspiring rebound from the 2011 flood) and the civic responsibility and gumption of their citizens. They are proud of their landscapes and farming heritage. They are proud to be hardscrabble, but also hip and progressive. We tell it to ourselves here in Vermont, but we tell it slant. We speak into the mirror and the mirror speaks back.

"It's the world's best foliage," says Frank, as he ambles down a sunlit path with his ponytailed business partner. He sits at a picnic bench under a canopy of leaves wearing a pink-striped polo shirt.

"The idea came to him one day when he was pondering everything that Vermont is known for," the reporter says, while on the screen Frank holds a baggie full of leaves up to the sun. *The world's best.* Then the camera cuts back to the two reporters in the studio. The reporter on the left is hugely pregnant.

"Guess I have a bunch of money hanging out in my backyard!" says the reporter on the right, a man, and they both chuckle as the screen fades to commercial.

* * * * *

The trail runs behind a bar. It's wooded and adjacent to a reedy marsh, often strewn with beer bottles and pieces of mud-soaked clothing: hats, T-shirts, gloves, the occasional pair of underwear. I hear the rush of I-89, which is about a half mile to my left and up a steep embankment, where a bridge traverses the river. I can smell the grease from the deli a block away—just a regular old deli serving chicken salad sandwiches and french fries. I skip over piles of old newspapers that clog up the little tributaries, making it hard for spawning salmon to swim upstream.

So when I see the squirrel in the middle of the path in front of me, splayed and dead, his white belly to the heavens and his four legs cast out in opposing directions, a near-perfect parody of death, his front right paw curling back over his heart; it is as if he had deposited himself there deliberately like a set prop, designed to startle me back into myself. Or perhaps he had been planted as a practical joke, so exactly centered in the path, and save for the one bent leg, completely symmetrical. How did he die? Suicide? A heart attack? Do squirrels have heart attacks? Do they topple from trees after spending millennia perfecting their acrobatics, only to shatter their spines in one eviscerating second, flouting the peaceable narratives we humans like to carry with us on our nature walks?

Black flies pour in and out of the squirrel's gaping throat and pace across his round, glassine eyes. They congregate near his nostrils, like coworkers around a water cooler, and occasionally dip a foot into the chasm, incessantly rubbing their two front legs together.

What does it mean when flies look like they are washing their front legs?
I'll ask the internet later.
Answer: *Washing their front legs.*

Other questions I've asked the internet recently:
Question: *Why do dogs walk in circles before lying down?*
Answer: *To tamp down ancient, invisible grasses to make a bed.*
Question: *How do you make a home?*
Answer: *Light candles!*

The trail is otherwise absent of humans, midday on a Wednesday, and I crouch in front of the carcass and recall an essay I've read recently—("Apologia" by Barry Lopez—in which he describes a drive from Oregon to Idaho to visit friends, stopping periodically to drag roadkill from the gravelly flanks of highways into the soft patches of brush or grasses, an impromptu burial, a small but reverent gesture.

"You never know," writes Lopez, "the ones you give some semblance of burial, to whom you offer an apology, may have been like seers in a parallel culture. It is an act of respect, a technique of awareness." I look at the dead squirrel's tiny, white teeth, aligned perfectly along his lower, distended jaw. I have the urge to run my finger along his downy throat and over the swell of his stomach, still warm, a siren of energy radiating out from his expired heart.

And then the dead squirrel shudders, gasps, and heaves. The flies knock their heads together in a frenzy to escape. I scream, seized with wonder, and grab the nearest sizable rock.

*   *   *   *   *

We countenance the world differently, my brother and me, but our impulses stem from the same well. I write to make sense of it, he gets high to forget it. We are both, so often, brought to our knees.

After the squirrel came back to life on the trail that day, I'd lifted the rock above my head, squeezed my eyes shut, and crushed his skull. My peripheral vision faded to gray. A single, pointless fly lay smashed beside the creature's brains, collateral damage. I picked up the rock and smashed the squirrel again. Then I did it again. I smashed the squirrel until all that remained was a pool of blood and bone, a kidney a foot away in the brush. The tiny, soft hairs inside one ear moved softly in the breeze. In a moment, the flies returned.

I survive, which means I can.

If the genesis of wonder is the sudden loss of what had once seemed self-evident, rendering the familiar strange, then it is the genesis of the addict, the artist, the mother, the sage, the pauper, the scientist, the priest, the child, the mortal, the magician, the living, and especially the dying.

The squirrel was dead, so I killed it.

"I put it out of its misery," I told Jack later. The party line.

Except that's not the whole story. And this is the part that haunts me even more than the ghosts of women and children. The squirrel proffered a question—*What are you capable of?*—and I answered from a deep reservoir of rage. After all, I had admired that mother mouse in the cabin trash can, so long ago, for her survival instincts. Marveled, even, at the severed heads of her pink, hairless offspring. So tiny and beautiful. Feats of engineering, really. Eyelids the size of a single chia seed. A dot of nose. The familiar rendered strange. Are those survival instincts not in me, too, an inheritance not only of grief but of a ruthless will to live? Is it Jack's question that haunts me still—*what if you give birth to an addict?*—or my own fear of the answer? I am terrified to mother a child who suffers as my brother suffers. I read somewhere that violent adults don't *become* violent; they only don't outgrow the violence of childhood. I still shudder to think of the violence I inflicted on my brother so long ago. And though I have largely outgrown it, I worry it is still burning inside me like a lodestar, guiding me toward my own imminent self-destruction. Yes, even here, in this placid, leaf-etched Vermont landscape, are razor-edged women trying to outrun themselves. Some of us succeed and some of us don't. It would be so easy, effortless even, to steer the car off the cliff. To hang grinning from tree branches. To abscond again and again, surviving as a grifter selling back to townspeople their own wares for double the price. Ultimately, there is no environment that can keep you safe from yourself. My brother taught me that. What's coming is already on its way. I imagine our own imminence like a razor blade poised over the delicate flesh of a fiery red maple leaf, aimed for the vein. You take a deep breath. You imagine all the beauty you can carve out of that smooth, delicate canvas. In your imagination, it's perfect, the masterpiece you will create. And yet you know it will be ruined—you've been warned, after all, *leaves decompose over time!*—and so you might as well make the first cut.

[DEEP PLAY]

It began in mystery, and it will end in mystery,
but what a savage and beautiful country lies in between.
—DIANE ACKERMAN

And then one day he's gone.

The end is as swift and merciless as the beginning was soft and
slow.

It is November of 2017, and we have been married for two years
and three months. We are thirty-three years old and have not
been apart for more than a couple weeks at a time during the
preceding fifteen years.

Perhaps you saw this coming. I did not.

When I say I am taken by surprise, I mean that the sky cracks
and shatters at my feet. I mean mountains moan in the distance then roar, unholy, as they plunge to the earth. I mean I am
lifted and flung headlong back onto the Island of Loss. The world
drains of color.

Of course, I am tempted to lay it all out; disembowel our private
pain, finger the bloody wreckage; label, pin it, and say, "Look.

Look." But in the end, the minutiae of his exodus are not important here, the various accusations and improprieties. It doesn't matter. Not anymore. I will say that he had made up his mind to leave long before I was even aware of its possibility. I can say how it felt, which is as if an entirely new person had invaded his body overnight. This new partner looked, smelled, and sounded just like my partner, but he was not my partner. My partner was not cruel. My partner did not look at me as if I were some gangrenous limb he needed to amputate in order to save his own life. My partner, I was sure of it, loved me.

It is the last night we will ever live together, though I don't know it yet, and he limps in after basketball practice, the community team he'd shocked us both by joining, and rolls around on the floor in front of the lit woodstove, writhing in pain. He groans and winces, clutching his knees to his chest. It's November and cold. The house hasn't yet absorbed the heat from the woodstove—the floors, walls, and furniture—and so there's no good place to lay your bones.

"Fuck," he groans. "Fuck, my back hurts."

The one-eyed dog runs gallant circles around him, trotting like a show horse. I smell his sweat evaporating in the heat. He takes off his socks and holds them out to the dog, who sniffs once then gingerly plucks them away. Jack groans again, says something about a new guy with aggression issues; something about a *pencil dick*; something about a *goddamn bullshit motherfucker*.

I watch these theatrics from the couch, baffled but strangely calm. Had someone told me in August, while we were riding our bikes along the craggy Maine coast, eating lobster rolls at McLoons Lobster Shack, swimming naked in David Pond, that by November my marriage would be ending, I would have blinked, turned, and walked away shaking my head. I would have called that person a goddamn bullshit motherfucker, maybe, and laughed merrily. But by late August he'd grown suddenly distant, mean even. I did not understand. It never occurred to me that he was grieving us. He stayed at work late and went to basketball twice a week now. We fought loudly about nothing while he retreated deeper and deeper into his computer at night. I'd wake up at two, three in the morning to pee and he'd still be downstairs. Crossing the hall, I'd glimpse the blue glow of his computer screen reflected in the window. I'd try to coax him to bed, but he'd refuse.

"Don't tell me what to do," he'd say.

And then there was that one night in September, shortly after the new semester had begun. We'd made dinner and lit candles, though I can't recall who had taken the initiative. I remember the window was open and the breeze carried the crisp, peaty smells of early autumn. Candles flickered. The one-eyed dog lay between us underneath the table, panting softly. We ate in silence, mostly, occasionally making half-hearted attempts at conversation. Something in our universe was about to shift and we both sensed it, I think. I was teaching a graduate class at Sarah Lawrence in New York that semester, my alma mater, so every Tuesday I'd drive the five hours south, spend the night in faculty housing on campus, teach all day Wednesday, and then drive the five hours back that evening. It was an arduous but interesting gig and I suppose it gave us both time to think. I don't remember now how it came up over dinner that night, but there it was again, the fly rematerializing in the ointment.

He didn't, wouldn't, have a child, he said. Not now. Not ever. He was only more certain. When he said it, he sighed and looked at me with both resolve and sympathy, like a doctor imparting a terminal diagnosis. I dropped my fork and it clattered to the floor. I was dimly aware of the dog licking my toes. Jack clenched his jaw. I remembered that when we were younger, he would suffer sudden, painful cramps in his joints as he grew into his adult body. "Here," he'd say, guiding my fingers to that spot on his jaw. I'd rub in circles and he'd exhale, sinking into my lap with his eyes closed. It felt like a triumph to tender him. His family wasn't physically affectionate, and it took a while for him to get used to it. He didn't like French kissing or too much nonsexual touching. For years, I'd feel him recoil when I tried to lick his lips or flick his tongue with my tongue. Eventually, he gave in or up, but I always sensed his slight displeasure in kissing or cuddling. After a visit with my family, he'd complain that I'd grown too accustomed to affection and would be extra needy, nuzzling into his body on the couch or hugging him too tightly. I'd laugh—it was true—but it also made me feel oafish in my affections, as if my love oppressed him. "I feel emotions," Jack told me once, "but they are like this," and he drew a straight, horizontal line on a piece of paper. "You feel like this," he said, and drew great, big waves across the page. Can a horizontal line really describe emotions, I wondered, when their defining feature is variability?

I got up from the table slowly and walked to the bathroom. There was nothing left to say. I didn't want to cry in front of him ever again. On the cold tile on the shower floor, I tried to breathe. I listened for his footsteps or the turn of the doorknob, but he didn't come. I turned on the water then turned it off. I lay back and put my legs in the air. My toes were painted a dark red, but I did not remember painting them. I tried again to figure out how to keep my marriage *and* have a child *and* make art *and* thwart death—mine, Eric's, my mother's, Jack's—but deep down I knew. No house, no garage, no job, no amount of sex or money or willful ignorance would keep this from happening, this inevitable cleaving. It was always coming.

*   *   *   *   *

I remember clearly the first shock of death. I was seven years old and sitting in a tide pool on a beach in New Jersey, the warm, stagnant water just covering my thighs while I traced vanishing lines through the wet sand between my legs. I don't know if it was the hum of my family's voices in the distance, or the undulant smack and shush of the waves, or the heat of the sun on my neck, or the evaporating marks I made in the sand, but suddenly I understood—violently, viscerally—that my life would end. I sensed the blankness of that, the black, and I slid onto my back in the belly of the salt-spunked water and let myself feel it.

It was the wonder in my childhood, and not the trauma, that I recall most vividly, and even then, I sensed that too much of it could be dangerous. Had the sands parted, had the universe opened and invited me back in, I would have gone joyfully. I would have let my body disassemble—made an offering of my kneecaps to the gulls—shallow bowls of flesh and brine. I would have drifted placidly back, back, and not fought dissolution. I'm sure of this. Decades later, during a precocious phase, I'll read *Passions of the Soul* by René Descartes and feel a flush of recognition: "But excessive wonderment, and astonishment at the sight of things that deserve little or no consideration, occurs far more frequently than its contrary. And this excess can entirely suppress or distort the use of reason." Too much wonder is not rational, he argues. It is a rapture of the deep, a lack of oxygen. The diver loses focus, succumbs to visions, cannot perceive nuance. In other words, too much wonder can render us awestruck or dumbstruck, depending on your point of view, but struck nonetheless. In the distance, my new universe sounded—the ocean waves, the wailing gulls, the scratch of hermit crab claws against the sand, my brother's voice pleading for ice cream. I woke to it slowly. I fought it until I couldn't fight it any longer. *I am alive*, I understood for the first time. *Hello*, I blinked wetly.

In rare and lucky moments, I still sense a rim of light around the edges of my consciousness. I spend a good deal of time trying to get back to that place of wonder, what Descartes calls "the first passion of all." Who does not suffer the primal trauma of being born, that first fragmentation, and who does not suffer it still? I learned in that moment, and cannot forget now, that the drive to self-obliterate is as powerful, if not more so, than the ambition to thrive. I tread this line every day. I read it into the smoldering lilac bush in the backyard, the faces of strangers, night sounds, even here in Vermont where it is very quiet. The world is so fragile, I think, so close to obliteration. Everywhere evidence of the quaking, shuddering sublime. Beauty and terror in the same breath. "I'm not even good at being tragic," one of my students said the other day. "I meant to take all of the pills, but only swallowed four. Then I laid on the floor in my underwear and hoped my partner got home in time to worry about me."

How else to say it? I smelled her neck one last time, our girl-child, Jack's and mine. I put my lips to her forehead. Her voice grew thin until it was only the shushing oscillations of the exhaust fan. She blinked once, twice, then out. On the bathroom floor, with my feet in the air, I watched our girl-child dissolve. I saw her age backward until she was just a tiny ball of cells inside me, amorphous and bright. Then I too began to shrink. We were a circle of light suspended inside my mother and her mother and her mother and her mother and her mother and her mother and her mother, all our mothers, all the way back to the beginning. I did not know where our body ended and theirs began.

We single star, we.

* * * * *

There's more to this divorce saga, of course, but it's interesting only in the way reality shows are interesting: as spectacle. Once, I picked up his boot and made to throw it at him. He flinched and I flung it at the wall. Once, he yelled that he'd fallen out of love with me, then took it back a moment later. Once, he told me that I'd taught him how to love, and I'd scoffed. "I've done a shitty job then."

"I'm moving out," he says that last night, still in a ball of pain on the floor in front of the woodstove, his forehead slicked with sweat. His eyes are bloodshot, and I realize he might have a fever, a virus, a tumor, something tangible to explain his behavior. Something more than the discrepancy over the kid, who I'd already wished away and mourned, on the bathroom floor that day in September, in order to save my marriage. Wasn't that enough?

For one last moment, I look at him. At us. The dog nips at his own tail. Outside, the stars shiver above the tree branches that clack against the living room window, trees that we *own*, part of the purchase of this small plot of land that backs to Thatcher Brook in a town called Waterbury, Vermont. What a thing to own a tree. Between the stars and the lake-bound bass twenty-five miles north of here—cold, white, and near-motionless in the belly of Lake Champlain—are invisible gold threads. Gold threads strung heart to heart between the bass and the stars; the stars and the past; the people and other people; the present and the future; the wild and the tame; the knowable and the unknowable. I imagine the threads are energy, struck and vibrating. They hold and connect and bind and occasionally pierce our wretched hearts.

Over there lays my long, old love with whom I have danced in snow, and dug through trash looking for something lost, and buried the bodies of our kin, and set up crooked Christmas trees, and lit the menorah, and bought rugs, and driven hours along highways in innumerable directions, and eaten a thousand egg rolls, and performed millions of *hellos* and *goodbyes* and *how was your days*, and held one another and turned our backs at night, and negotiated, and made lists and spreadsheets, and balanced budgets, and passed out drunkenly, and woken up mad, and cursed our mothers and fathers and brothers. We swam in oceans, lakes, and ponds together, our legs bumping. We've packed and unpacked our belongings in a half dozen different homes in five separate states. We've loved, and lied, and smelled one another's bad breath, and grown four or six tomato varietals in different patches of dirt with varying degrees of success. When I look at his face, he is simultaneously eighteen, and twenty-one, and twenty-five, and thirty, and thirty-three. He is a boy, casting alone into David Pond. He is an old man, casting alone into David Pond. Once, we leaped naked from an island of rocks into that same pond. We were nineteen. We held hands as we fell through the turpentine sky. It was the vast future, that sky, and the cold water below us flowed all the way back to our ancestors. We kicked our long, muscular legs and then scaled the rocks, asses to the sun, dirt and leaves and pine needles sticking to our shins and arms. We collapsed at the precipice, laughing. Maybe we had sex right there in the dirt, then leaped again into the cool water. Maybe we did it again and again and again.

*   *   *   *   *

It was play, our love then, "deep play" even, what the writer and scientist Diane Ackerman describes as "a combination of clarity, wild enthusiasm, saturation in the moment, and wonder." Once, Jack and I played together all the time. "To play is to risk," she says, "to risk is to play." We spend our lives in pursuit of these moments, these "altered states."

"Deep play," says Ackerman, "always involves the sacred and holy."

I nod, okay, and Jack looks away. The dog thumps to the floor beside him, panting contentedly in the stove's cedar heat and gnawing a sock. Once, when we were young, Jack had feared aloud that romance would ruin our friendship. It took fifteen years, but we did, finally, ruin it. But we'd also played, risked, and loved. I hold all of those contradictory truths in the same hand. That night, he sleeps on the couch and the next day he's gone, just like that. I'd taught him how to love, and now he was teaching me how to leave. I mean it when I say neither lesson was more important than the other.

*　*　*　*　*

And yet, what I think about most, two years later, are the women.

The women came slowly, then all at once. They came bearing suitcases and wine. They came and sat beside me and stayed for as long as I needed them.

Jessie arrives first, in late November, a few weeks after he moves out. I keep getting lost on my way to work, a fifteen-minute drive, then calling her crying. She's had enough. She drives through the night after work one day, eight hours and slightly stoned, to land on my porch at midnight. She roasts a chicken. We take long walks. We drive into the mountains and sit in the window at a hip farmhouse brewery. The stout is black and bitter. It has been six months since she was pregnant and then suddenly not-pregnant. We sit in the window and don't say much. The bartender has a cleft chin and a zebra tattoo on his forearm. Gray mountains stand sentry outside the window. A scrim of ache covers everything like dust. It's a silver limn that blinds me, a constant headache. In the silver field sits an empty silver chair. Silver children run in a circle around the chair, pushing each other over and shouting. November silvers the sky with heavy clouds. All sound is a silvering. Also, I am inexplicably attracted to the bartender. Inside the silver tunnel pulses a tiny thread of desire. Jessie drains her beer, grabs her purse, and pulls me up. "Get your silver shit together," she says. "Let's go."

In front of the hip brewery on top of the mountain in the middle of Vermont is the rest of the world. It spreads in all directions. Everything I once understood to be real feels very far away. I can't access it. I'm squinting a lot. I've heard talk of a cartoon villain as president, whispers that he's rousing ever more boils of hatred and violence, though I can't bring myself to follow the news. The other day, the college where I teach closed early after our students of color received threats in their mailboxes. There have been more mass shootings, Jessie tells me. Vegas. Sutherland, Texas. And yet my dumb, dissolving marriage is the only thing I can think about, the only topic worth discussing. It startles me to realize how selfish grief has made me. My grief looms so large I can't believe nobody else sees it. I feel my face is contorted into a constant expression of pain, as if I've had a stroke, but nobody comments. "Is my left eye drooping?" I ask Jessie. Everywhere, other people are suffering and dying, but what about my vanished husband, I demand. How Jessie can stand me is a marvel.

"How I can stand you is a marvel," she says.

"Don't take this the wrong way," he texted a couple days ago. It was the first communication in three weeks. "But how's the dog?" He was worried about me too, he explained, but he'd been having nightmares about the dog and it was interrupting his sleep. He wanted me to say that the dog was depressed, that he mooned all day in the window, watching for his car, which was true but not what I told him.

"Dead," I wrote back.

Jessie drives us home while I stare out the window at the tunnel. "I hate who this divorce has made me," I whine.

"You're grieving," she says. "It's a survival mechanism. You're focusing your energy on the wound so that it can heal. The fucking asshole." I believe her. I always believe her. Especially the fucking asshole part, which she's started to use like punctuation.

"Did he take *all* the pillows, the fucking asshole?"

"Fucking asshole, if he dares show up here, I'll kill him, the fucking asshole."

"Here's your coffee," she says in the morning, then walks away shaking her head. "The fucking asshole."

When we were teenagers, our love lives detonated daily. We'd drive around crying and getting stoned. A single day contained whole eras. Hours bloomed with possibility and despair. When my father died when I was seventeen, and Jessie moved into my bedroom without a word, centuries passed before we left the house again. Time ballooned around us. We could not find its edges, so we sat there and blinked and waited for our lives to change.

Here we are again, driving and getting stoned. It has been so long since I've been stoned that it feels like nothing, or I cannot tell being stoned apart from the tunnel. It is today and twenty years ago and fifty years hence. She rolls down the windows and plays Led Zeppelin and we are simultaneously girl-children and old women. Her thin, dark hair stands straight up in the wind and she drums on the steering wheel. We are here and there and everywhere at once.

✳   ✳   ✳   ✳   ✳

So many words, but never the right ones to tell her how much I love her; how much of my identity is because of and in relation to her. There is no readily available language for this love—the love between female friends—no institution through which we might affirm and commit ourselves. Once, women declared their love for one another boldly. Middle-class Victorian women, for example, wrote their girlfriends florid letters of devotion ("Susie, forgive me Darling, for every word I say—my heart is full of you. . . . Yet when I seek to say to you something not for the world, words fail me," wrote Emily Dickinson to her beloved sister-in-law and friend, Susan Gilbert), and wore jewelry woven from one another's hair. Not so lovely were the waxed neon friendship bracelets Jessie and I made out of gimp in the 1990s, but the sentiment was the same. Once, women hugged and kissed one another indiscriminately. They held hands as they strolled down the street and through parks. They shared wild imaginings, musings, gossip, desires, and curiosities. Before marriage took precedence as the primary emotional relationship of one's life, around the mid-1900s, intimacy between women was often more important than the affectionate respect many felt for their husbands. Men shared these bonds with one another too. It wasn't considered gay to fall asleep beside one's same-sex friend, or even tangled in their arms, though of course homosexual relationships were as common then as they are now.

I'm not extolling the Victorian era as a heyday for women, but practices in kinship then were more in line with how *Homo sapiens* evolved. We are essentially a tribal species, and for the vast majority of our history, the tribe was the primary unit, not the nuclear family. We were bound by generations of kinship and cooperation. In fact, for a long time it was considered wildly antisocial to be too emotionally attached to one's spouse. Social and economic interdependence meant that bonds with one's friends, neighbors, and communities was essential. They provided emotional, financial, and physical sustenance. Until the mid-nineteenth century, the word "love" was relegated to friendship bonds, and not typically used in reference to one's spouse.

We know the rest of the story. Agriculture settled us into communities, and the Industrial Revolution piled us into cities. But it wasn't until after World War II that we splintered into suburbs and began prizing the nuclear family over all other bonds. It serves capitalism, after all, to live so divided. To work hard for the betterment of our own lives and the lives of our children to the exclusion of our communities, neighbors, and friends. This is not to say that we ought to look to our nomadic, tribal days as more or less "natural" than we way we live now, but it's a good reminder that we are not wired for isolation, biologically or neurologically.

I must be stoned after all because I babble on about this to Jessie. I've been doing research for an essay about female friendship and I'm suddenly desperate to tell her about it. That she understands this deeply is urgent, like the time we were on mushrooms in high school and I needed her to understand that pineapple could cure cancer. I tell her that sometime in the early to mid-twentieth century, friendships, especially between women, were now viewed as a threat to marriage's primacy. Same-sex friendships were newly suspicious. The so-called Golden Age of Marriage post–World War II meant middle-class married couples were suddenly expected to fulfill most of one another's emotional needs for the first time in history. And yet despite huge social changes over the last century, the residue of this social stigma remains.

"Remember when Mom asked us if we were gay because we shared my bed every night?" I ask her. She nods. "Like that," I say.

I never believed a romantic partner could or should be a one-stop shop for all our emotional needs, but I received the message too—that once we find true love, we ought to retreat into marital bliss and commit ourselves wholly to its preservation. It's a myth that persists through evolving understandings of feminism, sexuality, gender, and gender roles, and it has never been more evident to me than in this moment—my lover gone and my friend here, passing me a joint and holding my hand as we drive through the mountains. What is the difference between this love and my love for Jack, really, when it comes down to it? I want to find this variable and study it under a microscope.

Which love is more valuable, and how do we define love's value anyway? And from what vantage point? Today? Next year? On the cusp of death?

We ask too much of our lovers. That they be our best friend and confidant and financial partner and coparent and entertainer and emotional supporter and caretaker and lover and our equal in domestic responsibilities, and through it all they must practice unwavering loyalty. Isn't it a bit much? And yet nobody anticipates getting divorced at thirty-three. It's no one's goal. It's a momentous failure. It's embarrassing. It's unladylike.

"It's inevitable," says Jessie. "You can't be everything to one person for fifteen years and not fucking resent them for it."

She looks startled at the wisdom of her own words, then for good measure adds, "The fucking asshole."

*   *   *   *   *

Walking is the only thing I do well now. It tethers me. I fear that if I stop moving, I will dissolve inside the grief. I walk and listen to podcasts or audiobooks. Stories get me out of my own head. There are never enough stories. Reading is hard for the first time in my life—too much silence, which leaves a gap for my own thoughts—but with my headphones on everything else is drowned out. The one-eyed dog loves this new development. We walk every morning and evening. On days I don't have to teach, we walk three, four times a day. We walk for many miles at a time, the same route that the husband and I used to walk together. Left across the little bridge that traverses Thatcher Brook, right onto Lincoln Street, past the Park and Ride, then veer left onto the Waterbury Community Path and out of sight of the farmhouse where one day I sat on the porch and cried in frustration because the one-eyed dog refused to get back on his leash and instead ran circles around me for hours, unseduced even by the enraged squirrel stuck in the squirrel trap on the porch stoop. An old man cracked open the door, saw me weeping leash in hand, nodded, and then pulled the door closed again, as if weeping women landed on his doorstep every day and what was he to do about it? After the farmhouse, the path continues through the woods at a steady incline, then onto a small, gravel, dead-end street, after which it continues through Western Hills Golf Course. The terrain here is predictably hilly, and I climb fast and hard through strong winds. Over the past year I've watched this landscape evolve through each season. The path is surrounded by fields of wildflowers that eventually cede to manicured greens. It is an honor to watch the same patch of land dress and undress over time—the long-necked trillium and white-bellied trout lilies of early spring; summer's wild lupine, violet and straight-backed; bright yellow Indian blanket in August; then in fall the goldenrod, asters, and the Queen Anne's lace that lure the butterflies who then bait the dog with their bravado. Come November, these fields are stalked, dry, and mustard yellow; then mowed flat for winter. December covers them gently with blankets of blue snow, which freeze tight as a straitjacket by January and remain through April.

Today I climb the highest hill and look east to where a long, winding road leads toward the husband's new apartment. On the side of the road is a little white farmhouse beside which a boy in yellow pants kicks around a ball by himself—the pants are striking against so much brown. An ambulance rushes past the farmhouse in the direction of the apartment and for a moment I hope it's headed there, not for anything serious—a broken toe, maybe, or knuckles cracked from punching the wall in despair—so that I'd be summoned to the hospital by a well-meaning receptionist calling for his wife. "I'm his wife," I'd say, and race to sit beside his bed, looking concerned and luminous when he awoke from the morphine drip (do they give morphine drips for broken knuckles?), my hand stroking his cheek.

The fantasy cuts out there, because I can't decide what I'd like to happen next. Months of rehabilitation during which I'd steadfastly martyr myself in hopes that he'll realize that breaking up our marriage was a grave mistake? For him to grovel and beg for my forgiveness? To be able to shrug and leave him there after he learns he'll have to wear a cast on each hand for six months and won't be able to hold his own penis?

But it doesn't matter what I want. He's gone and the ambulance continues around the mountain. The siren fades and the lonesome boy in yellow pants goes back to his ball.

*   *   *   *   *

Hannah comes and Aryn comes and Rya comes and Kara comes and John with an H comes all the way from D.C. in an airplane. Sometimes they come alone and sometimes they come together and sometimes I don't want them to come and other times I want them to come but don't know how to ask and then they're just there like magic. Like a tribe.

*   *   *   *   *

My mom arrives in December and one night Hannah and Aryn come over and the four of us eat a huge meal that we make together. After dinner, I grab a pile of sheets to make up the couch for Aryn, but I trip over them and fall down the stairs. I land in a heap at the bottom and the women gather around me like a shroud. The tunnel collapses and all I feel is grief. All of it at once. I cry and they hold me. The dog circles us suspiciously while a bruise, the biggest and blackest I've ever seen, blooms on my right hip. Later, they help me upstairs and into pajamas. They help me ease into bed and roll me into the middle. Then Aryn slips in on my left and Hannah on my right. They sleep on either side of me that night, like buffers, and occasionally I wake up crying and one or both of them will put a hand on my back or stroke my arm until I fall back asleep.

Almost nightly, my mom and I have dance parties in the living room. "Dance," she demands when I start panicking. "Just get up and dance." One night, she takes a video of me dancing to "Ooh La La" by the band Faces and yelling, "I'm reclaiming music!" We never danced together before, but suddenly it feels imperative, like the only way to shake out the pain. It feels sacred, like play, this new ritual of ours. In fact, one of the origins of the word "play" is the Anglo-Saxon word *playa*, which means to sing or dance, but the original meaning is more perilous. In Indo-European, *plegan* means to risk, chance, expose oneself to hazard. "Play's original purpose was to make a pledge to someone or something by risking one's life," says Ackerman, which sounds a lot like marriage, and also awe's intrinsic underbelly: terror. In the video, I am newly thin from all the walking. My ponytail flaps around and my sweatpants hang from my hips. We've rearranged the living furniture in some vain attempt to make the place feel more like mine. I sleep in the guest room now and wake up every morning in a panic, unsure of where I am, until the knifing sorrow returns. I've taken down his painting of the lumberjack and stuffed it in a closet. Every morning, I lug piles of wood inside to keep the woodstove burning. I use his mail as kindling. That night, I dance so wildly that a mirror behind me falls off the wall and shatters and I scream out in surprise.

I still have no idea where I'll go or what I'll do. The image that keeps coming to mind is that of a plane circling overhead in a holding pattern. But for now, I live in the blue house on the hill and I own half of it, along with half of the trees and half of the dead garden and half of that crumbling garage. I drink and dance and leap over shattered glass and everywhere things are falling.

*   *   *   *   *

January and it's been two months since he left. What surges in me now is an inexplicable lust. I want to fuck every man I see, as if I am eighteen again. It reminds me of something my mother told me once, that for days after each of her forced abortions, she was overcome by lust. It was as if her body was compelling her to replace what had been lost. The "life instinct," she called it. And though the stakes are not the same, the impulse feels familiar, as if my body will not succumb to the grief in my mind. As if my body is rebelling against the dimming prospects of motherhood. It feels both physiological and primal. When the life instinct kicks in, it feels a lot like puberty all over again, replete with the attendant depression, confusion, and shame, though thankfully sans acne and aching breasts. And so now it is walking and women and stories and sexual fantasies with the gas station attendant that keep me afloat. I head to Nebraska for ten days to teach my graduate students. Here, too, women comfort me, my friends and fellow faculty—Teri, Karen, Amy, Liz, Charlene—they send flowers to my room and Karen lends me her car so I can go get a massage one morning from her friend, a healer who lives fifteen minutes away in a suburban subdivision and touches me so tenderly I cry silently into the massage bed. On New Year's Eve, Karen conducts tarot card readings in her room. The faculty wait our turn and in the meantime drink and chat in small groups. Karen is all grace, silver-haired and calm. Her perfume smells like butter and thyme. Around us, conversations vibrate. Charlene hands me a glass of wine and lets me rest my head on her bosom. I feel newly like a child with these wise women, my colleagues, and I don't care. They know that heartbreak is a kind of death too. I let myself be tendered. Their kindness is a gift and I fight the conviction that I do not deserve it. Afterward, instead of going downstairs to the party, I go to bed. If I have to listen to "Auld Lang Syne" and watch people make out I might never recover. It's eleven o'clock and a text comes in from my eighty-five-year-old Mommom: "I'M AT A PARTY RIGHT NOW!" That's it, no other context, so instead of crying, I close my eyes and imagine her swinging from chandeliers.

Back in Vermont, I start furiously applying for full-time teaching jobs. The husband wants to buy me out of the blue house on the hill and at first I'm angry and then relieved. It's the middle of winter in Vermont and everywhere looks like sadness made manifest. Gone, the romantic beauty of snow-capped mountains and steaming chimneys. All that remains are the cracked ribs and encroachment I noted during that first drive up 89 North upon moving here in January seven years ago. Here, in this frozen tundra of doom. Back then, I'd barreled toward him, sure that our love would keep us both safe. Now, all I wanted was to leave him, and Vermont, behind.

*   *   *   *   *

Here's what April brings along with her showers:

A lawyer so unsentimental I shoot tea out of my nose when she tells me to leave him with his limp dick in his hand and not look back.

A therapist so unflinching she takes my call at ten at night while I'm having a panic attack and then calls me back two hours later to make sure I'm okay.

A job offer at a small liberal arts college outside of Columbus, Ohio.

April 16, 2018: the results from an anatomy scan that show a perfectly round head, as big as her father's, and all her lovely, intact bones. Jessie's second pregnancy, a girl-child five months cooked, is thriving.

*   *   *   *   *

Here's what I remember. When I was young, I understood this world to be a porous veil over the other world, the one we came from and the one to which we return, endlessly, in some sort of cosmic loop. I glimpsed the other world often, while playing down by the creek in our neighborhood, in bed at night in half--sleep, while curled in my mother's lap in the early morning. It is hard to describe now as an adult because whatever connection I felt to this other world has dimmed, the portal has been eclipsed. Before the age of seven, sensory information is like Play-Doh: endlessly pliant. Without drugs or a serious medita-tive practice, our sensory experiences as adults are more fixed. But children are closer to the black that comes before and the black that comes after. And at a certain point, *because who can live and feel so much?*, the knowledge fades, the connection severs (we see ourselves in the mirror, literally and figuratively), and we spend the rest of our lives trying to get back to our place of be-ginning—where we felt ourselves connected to the whole. If this resembles spiritual narratives, perhaps it is because the narra-tive line contains implicit truths, even if the particulars remain subject to endless debate. Call it god, call it love, call it arche-types, call it play, call it poetry, call it wonder, call it grace. There are no exclusions. It is & and & and & and & and.

[IN THE END,
WE ALL BECOME STORIES:
LAST LETTERS TO JACK]

It is considered axiomatic that pain depends on
consciousness, so a demonstration that fishes can feel pain
depends on showing that they are also conscious.

—from *Fish and Fisheries*, 2013

I.
MARCH 12, 2017

Dear Jack,

I watched you wrestle the bass, gripping the base of the tail with
your free hand. It was May 2, 2016, about eighteen months before you left. On that day you harnessed the fish by pressing your
thumb firmly into his distended lower jaw, then dislodging the
hook from the gills, fist-deep in his throat. A line of thinned
blood rivered through his scales, then splashed on the tops of
your bare feet. It was early spring; clusters of horseflies conti-
nented the surface of the water. I squatted beside the pond and
peed but kept you in my sightline. I was worried about you and
you knew it. You would not look at me. Dropping the rod on the
grass, you splayed him out on the picnic table where he bucked
and slapped—one lidless, dilated eye fixed to the sky. The fish
did or did not feel pain. We were thirty-two years old and had

been married for a year. With the exception of this one, I was spending every weekend that spring house-hunting. The day before this one, your father died. He fell off a ladder onto a concrete driveway and hit his head, after which he survived in a coma for four days.

You were fishing because a) it calms you; b) you wanted to inflict pain to avoid feeling pain; c) you believe the spectacle of pain is the same as pain itself; d) all of the above. I still don't know the answer.

"The eyes of the largemouth glow when he feeds," you told me once, and I envisioned the waters electric at night, flash-lit, mirroring the fireflies in the sky; coded conversations between them.

"I don't think that's how it works," you'd said.

But what do we call responses to pleasure except love?

Your father did not teach you how to fish. You learned small and quiet along the banks of David Pond while behind you he shellacked the smooth, tanned pine boards that would become the stairs to the camp's refinished loft. You love fishing largemouth for the fight, the slow circuitous stalking of prey before the strike, the water around the line swelling, then echoing out into larger and larger half-moons, the line spinning out as the fish arrows into the belly of the lake.

For four days, we hovered around his hospital bed while nurses came and went, shining flashlights into his pupils. The light waves entered and were swallowed. He did or did not feel pain. Doctors had removed a piece of his skull to reduce the swelling in his brain, but scans illuminated (on the bright screen in the dim room) whorls of gray like a churning hurricane. Like a stirred pot. Like a thousand indecent metaphors, each one less comprehensible than the last. The room glowed blue, which anyway he couldn't see.

I bought bagels no one could eat until they did. In millimeter increments, cans of Liquid Hope® were deposited into your father's stomach via a feeding tube. You went to the bathroom to pee, and in your daze, forgot to tuck yourself back into your pants. You held a long and stoic conversation with a young nurse about your father's increasingly futile treatments, sitting on the window seat that doubles as a guest bed, where your mother would later collapse from fatigue—literally collapse, like a marionette severed from her strings—afternoon half-light streaming past your shoulders while you glanced back and forth between the nurse and the red, climbing digits on the brain pressure monitor. The nurse stood in front of you, and when the conversation was over, nodded once, briskly, at your crotch before walking away, leaving you staring down at your soft and senseless cock and thinking only, *Oh*.

You read the age of the fish in the rings around his scales. Six years (a tenth of your father's natural life) nearly half of which has likely been spent near-motionless at the bottom of the pond. The average lifespan of a largemouth bass is sixteen years, which is the amount of time between when my father fell to his death and yours. The similarities end there, though.

Your father was dead and I was hungry. It would be indecent to kill and eat that fish, I knew; instead, you held him tenderly in the shallows beside the dock, rocking him back to life, one gill gaping and torn, until he shivered violently, once, and then disappeared.

They pumped saline into his veins in the hopes that he would float.

They kept the glacial cap of his skull chilling in a refrigerator.

Nurses pinched his toes and fingers, bent his thumb backward against the hard ridge of a pen, but he did not flinch.

With our intact brains, we imagined and reimagined his fall, the sound of his skull smacking against the concrete.

On the driveway, a moon of blood bloomed and bloomed.

After he died, we slept in the loft your father built, inside the same pool of time that contained the bass and the bed and the brain so swollen his eyes bulged beneath his eyelids. In two days, the bruises lightened and disappeared. *What a strong body*, the nurses commented, *what a healthy heart*. When they peeled back his lids, his eyeballs were round and wet and fixed in place. He lay motionless and we baited him from above, but he would not surface.

Forgive me: I do not mean to force the metaphor.

Only—when the nurses finally removed the lines from his veins, the tube from his gaping mouth, and the room hummed with fear while he stiffened, gasped, then cooled—his skin waxed yellow and I was stupid hungry and you were a wet, shook thing I wanted to take inside the dark of my mouth.

Instead, we gathered up our belongings: blankets, jackets, extra underwear, candy wrappers, water bottles, Chapstick, and tissues—all the wastes of the living—and drove to the house where your father used to live. For dinner, we ate the beans he had made in the Crock-Pot the morning of his fall, stewed in sliced onions and brown sugar, which a neighbor had put away in the refrigerator. We ate and ate and ate and when there was nothing left to eat, we tossed the Styrofoam bowls into the trash can, drove to the pond, cast into the water, and braced our bodies for the strike.

II.
APRIL 30, 2017

Dear Jack,

When you were a boy in Maine, you took your red-striped fishing rod out into the yard—neon yellow bobber electric against the opaque gray sky—and cast into a puddle of snowmelt and waited. Brown fields, early spring, early morning. No one around for miles, except your mother in the kitchen window smiling to herself, and the dog, Bob, who one day soon, at twenty years old, will lay down on the driveway for a nap and die, accidentally run over by your father in his haste and old truck, the dog's tail thrashing wildly against the gravel, reflex and not joy, while you watch stricken from the patio.

I envision you a small, six-year-old boy, as you slowly reel in your line through clumps of dead grass, because a body of water, a puddle broken overnight even, surely must contain fish. Water-blue eyes, sandy-bottom hair, your pants overlarge yet too short, barefoot boy in April. You fish until dusk, then slump over your spaghetti dinner, dreaming storks scooping bass from nearby ponds and dropping them into swimming pools in distant, wealthier neighborhoods—a story you'd heard once from you-can't-remember-who and taken to heart. You won't accept your empty fishing creel by your feet, and keep lifting its woven hatch to check, while old Bob curls around your ankles, weightless as blown grass.

And yet, to this day, I'm not sure you fully understand the stranglehold of story. Because Eric was a boy and all the addicts in our family were men, I explained to you once, he was cast as the future addict by the time he was five years old. In the story of our little family, I was the good girl, the overachiever, the one who would keep it together. And so I did. The story demanded it. It demanded other things, too, things I am still trying to unravel.

But one of those things was that I stave off chaos with careful control. You became part of that need for control, and I pulled and wrenched you through our twenties with a willful sense of purpose. Another of those things was that I become a mother. I grew increasingly determined to fulfill that ambition before I ever questioned whether it belonged to me or The Women. Rather than harness my ambivalence, I tried to tame it, to turn it into a story about ghosts—because if anything has more narrative power than love, it's our wounds.

But this is not that story.

Once, you were a superstitious boy. You believed in the magic of storks and wearing the same pair of socks to every basketball game. Of putting on your clothes in a certain order, pants always last. But you never caught that fish, you lost games, and by the time we met in college, you were convinced we'd ruin our friendship by trying for something more. And this has been your approach to most everything ever since. *If I expect the worst, I can only be pleasantly surprised.* That was a story about your wounds.

This is not that story, either.

When I try to understand why you changed your mind about us having kids seven months before our wedding—*I thought I would want them one day*, you'd said finally, *I didn't know*—I think about the stories we tell ourselves about ourselves; if this sort of storytelling manifests the future or threatens it. I never considered an alternative narrative to motherhood. And so I felt you'd erased two souls from the banks of my horizon: the child I'd hoped to have and the mother I was always becoming. I keep lifting the hatch of my mind, searching for a story that might contain a happy and childless ending. But all story is magical thinking. The only difference between your superstitions and my faith in story is nothing much. They both assume a sense of control we do not possess. Funny to think of it now, now that enough time has passed that such memories can be funny again, how often I would ask you in the moments before sleep, "Tell me a story," by which I meant a story of who you were before I knew you. Eventually, of course, you ran out of stories. For a while, a few years, you'd retell stories I'd heard before, greatest hits, requests, like the one about losing your virginity in a cabin; or how you would secret *Highlights* magazines into the makeshift mailbox of your fort in the woods just so you could delight in discovering mail the next day; or when your cousin killed himself by driving his motorcycle into a Mac truck; or your father's uncontrollable rages and your mother's silent ones. But my favorite was this: the boy fishing alone in a puddle in his front lawn. Funny to realize now what I was really asking for all those nights before sleep, when I whispered "Tell me a story" into your warm neck. As if I could read your stories like tea leaves the future we were creating, the child we would make, the life we would cultivate day by day.

Here is a story I never told you.

This one takes place 457 miles and 15 years south of here and goes I was in love with a different boy I'll call S. I was 12 when we first met, and he was 14, and we lived in the same neighborhood. S. was sad most all of the time. And you know, don't you? How I've always loved solemn boys. This one wore a long, blue overcoat and knocked on my door every evening for ten years— "Jess, S. is here," my mother would call, "Again."—and we'd sit on the front stoop toeing the gravel driveway for hours while it grew dark and then darker. We were going to get married and have children and I would make him whole and well (already, you can predict how this story will end). But then he left me and the neighborhood for the army at age eighteen, two weeks before his mother killed herself and no one was surprised. He circled my dreams for years (years after I also left the neighborhood for good, and met you, and we married)—S.'s hands on my face inside the rooms in which we took the same drugs together as teenagers—and I would wake up thrashing until you opened the curtains to the sun and said, *Look*.

You might not understand that it's the story, and not the boy, that haunts me. The real boy—a man now living in New York City—is not, has never been, who I wanted him to be. Just a character in my story, and me in his, until we found one another again a few years ago and he finally told me what I'd always wanted to hear, inside that dark bar in our old neighborhood—*I love you, I've always loved you*—tall and tattooed and army-strong. You and I were separated then, the only time we'd separated before this final one, four terrible months a few years before we married. In that dark moment S.'s confession had felt like destiny, like a reason for all the pain of losing you. He pulled me up from my chair and kissed me hard. It felt wonderful and familiar and warm. It felt like something we deserved for all the years apart.

What happens when an angry boy goes to war? I wondered. "You wouldn't want to see me unmedicated," S. warned.

The insinuation was violence, innate and uncontrollable, and though I did not push for more information I knew he was not exaggerating. I had sensed rage in him from long ago and knew intuitively that his decision to join the army at eighteen was driven by a ferocious desire for power and violence born from childhood traumas he never spoke about but that floated in the air around him. Between us. And yet, toward me he had only ever been kind and gentle. I knew those conflicting identities to be equally true, and yet still he was a puzzle I would never solve, and no doubt that was why he haunted me all those years.

But at the hotel room later, he couldn't look at me while we had sex. His dick was very big, I discovered, and because I was angry, I imagined telling you about it later, though of course I never did.

I never told you any of this. Afterward, I stroked his arm, tracing the curves of an elaborate tattoo. He flinched, and I realized he didn't want me to touch him like that, tenderly, I suppose. "What are you doing?" he asked me, but I didn't have an answer. "I'm sorry," I said, and took my hand away. He'd sighed and rubbed his eyes then. The closeness I'd felt to him moments before evaporated, and in the starkness of our emptied desire and the tawdry hotel room, I knew suddenly it was not me he loved but the story of us: childhood sweethearts reunited on the other side of years and the war he'd fought. Broken halves who together make a whole. *You were meant to be*, the story insists. *You were always in the process of becoming*. When I watched that truth bear down on him in the seconds that followed, it was as crushing to both of us, I think, as any death. In the morning, I sat naked on the bed and watched him gather his clothes. His black hair was spackled tight to his head and his body looked spit-shined. I hugged my knees, my hair tangled, and my breasts pressed flat to my thighs. He paused, turned to face me, and said, "You look like you just got fucked," and in that instant decades of shame bore down on me at once and he grinned.

But the night before, after we'd kissed, we'd sipped our beers in silence while the bartender shouted up the stairs, *last call*, and we'd toasted. How I wish I could say the story ended there. That we finished our beers inside that silence and left. That he hadn't told me then—in the dark bar in our old neighborhood, gazing down at my knees, a sudden source of wonder, while all the old narratives began to reassemble in the space between his lips and my thighs—about leaving basic training all those years ago to collect his mother's ashes and carry out her final wish: her feather-light urn to the shores of the Atlantic, bearing it aloft and alone into the wind and waves and letting fly her flaked ashes, food for the fishes, into the roiling and indifferent sea. But here's the thing about wishes: they can only *become* true and are not inherently so. Her suicide note had read like a job resignation. ("My circumstances have changed," I remember him quoting.) In her place, she had appointed him, her youngest son, S., to care for his siblings. Later he learned the unthinkable, that his uncle, her brother, had secretly buried his sister—*We're Catholics, for Christ sake!* the uncle later argued—and the ashes S. had scattered were just his uncle's old dog. How I wish I could release him from that fact, unsee his face when it told it to me in the bar that night.

I was reading a book by Margaret Atwood around this time, and I'd copied down a quote on a piece of notebook paper that I'd pinned above my desk: "In the end, we'll all become stories." She did not say we *are* stories, or even that we *create* stories, which would imply false agency, I think. Instead, she wrote: "All that anxiety and anger, those dubious good intentions, those tangled lives, that blood. I can tell about it or I can bury it." I know you would prefer that I bury it. The story we became, after all, is as plain and ordinary as the pine desk you made me years ago, which is where I write to you now. Except I can still read history in the wood grain, and smell the dust on your fingers as we stood in the kitchen, a pot of chili on the stove and your hands in my hair.

Inside the hatch of my mind, I slip a fish into the puddle while your back is turned, before you toddle away crestfallen for dinner. How I wish those tiny tugs on your line had been real and not just hope for a happy ending, a hook tangled in grass. I can't help but think of this boyhood story as the last of your optimism, feeble as it might seem, except I know the power of story. How ten thousand years ago, hyenas stacked human bones by the bushel. But then we invented language, heroes, stories. We told lies about men defeating saber-toothed tigers until they really could. We imagined surviving and then we survived.

You imagined loving me until you did.

———

I know that story fails us half of the time. There is no viable story to make sense out of the senselessness of war, for example, or the rewriting of a woman's final chapter. I cannot write S. into wellness, just as I cannot will a child alive. I know this now.

But when I asked you, time and again, *Are you sure . . . ?* I was asking you not to give up on the miraculous. I was raging against the inevitability of entropy, the limits of our own self-narratives.

I was saying: *I do not accept it.* The acting of salvation *is* salvation.

I was saying: In the end, we'll all become stories.

And I am telling you now, he was happy, your old haggard dog. In those final moments, cast out from the confines of a body, he was ecstatic.

[CLEAVE]

When her diagnosis comes, it is not a shock. When the right superior lobe of her lung is removed, analyzed, and eventually incinerated, we are strangely calm. It was inevitable. We knew it was coming and, perversely, believed it would be okay. It feels like this—impersonal and at a distance. Anything but a swift and complete recovery is unfathomable and so we speak of "the surgery," "the problem," even sometimes "the cancer," but never "her cancer" or "lung cancer," which would be to admit the possibility of her mortality, which is unacceptable. They'll remove the lobe containing the cancer, adenocarcinoma of the lung, which we keep telling people is the "cancer you want to have if you have to get cancer," although we have no hard evidence to support this claim. The tumor is small, and if surgery goes well, she may not need radiation or chemotherapy, but we won't know until after the surgery.

It's May of 2019. I drive to Philadelphia from Columbus. I've just finished my first year of teaching at Denison and I'm in love with my new city, students, and colleagues. I feel unspeakably lucky to have landed here. Even if the position is technically temporary, I'm hopeful.

The women gather. Mommom, Aunt Carole, my mother's many friends, Jessie and her long-lashed girl-baby, Jules, six months old and a ferocious hair-puller. Here too is Eric, sober for six months, the longest stretch of sobriety he's thus far maintained. In the days leading up to the surgery, we play cards and eat. We gather supplies. Pajamas. Pillows. Soft things. I make soups and freeze them. We plant her a garden and I build an outdoor lounge chair from IKEA that takes six hours and sixty screws. The recovery period will be anywhere from four to six weeks and she'll need a place to rest outside. She eyes me bringing in more bags of groceries. "I'm making kale salads, butternut squash soup, and vegetable stew," I declare.

"This isn't wartime, you know," she says. "You'll still be able to go to the grocery store after the surgery."

"Yes, but we'll be very busy convalescing," I tell her.

"You mean me," she says. "You mean I will be very busy convalescing."

"You, me, we. Same thing."

She hasn't had a cigarette in two months, and I can't stop smelling her. She smells like sunbaked crackers and salt. Like someone I distantly recall but can't quite summon.

In the pre-op room, we gather around her bed to stroke her hair and kiss her and ask the doctors questions we've already asked a hundred times. We smile and act like she's taking a little vacation, not heading into surgery to have a part of her lung removed.

"Isn't he cute?" she says to me, pointing at the young anesthesiologist who stands at the computer clicking keys and turning red.

"Adorable," I say. "He's also married," I tell her, noting the ring. "Now let the guy do his job."

We are a gaggle, a brood. Mommom, Aunt Carole, Eric, and me.
We prattle and moon. We joke. We are in the way. We go back to
the waiting room.

✱   ✱   ✱   ✱   ✱

Later, while she's in surgery, we go to the cafeteria and eat sandwiches and drink coffee. Eric goes outside to smoke and doesn't
come back for a long time, which nobody else notices. It is eight
o'clock in the morning and it's going to be a long day. Outside,
food trucks line the avenue and people stand around in scrubs
or tool belts or suit jackets. They drink coffee or smoke or stare
at their phones or yell at their dogs. Was it a year ago already?
Eric, pale, bloated, and floating atop a different hospital bed, covered in white sheets and mostly incoherent when we showed up.
A week prior, an employee at the Rite Aid Pharmacy across the
street from the hospital had discovered him face down in the
bathroom, overdosed and unconscious, and called 911. The para-
medics gave him three doses of Naloxone and performed CPR before he came to, and still he'd barely survived. The woman he'd
been with that night, Frances, had picked him up from the Philadelphia Corrections Facility the day before, where he'd served
out his time for the robbery. She'd dropped him off at the hospital emergency room only hours before because they'd been doing coke all day and he told her he wanted to go into detox. But instead of going into the hospital, he'd crossed the street, entered
the pharmacy, purchased a package of needles intended for use
by diabetics, and barricaded himself in the bathroom with a bag
of dope. Frances, a forty-seven-year-old mother of two, left him at
the hospital entrance, drove the twenty minutes to her New Jersey
home alone, and a few hours after returning, overdosed and died.

Over a year later, and after nine months of sobriety, Eric says:

*I'm only just now starting to feel anything about Frances's death.
I guess because I'm sober. I'm feeling a lot of guilt. The other day*

I woke up in my own room [at the halfway house where he's liv-
ing] and sure, it's in the basement, which is unfinished, the ceil-
ing is still just drywall and there's only a little pink throw rug,
but I woke up and I thought, "I've never had it so good." And that
made me feel awful because even though I guess I deserve it, I
don't know if I deserve it, if that makes sense. Fran killed her-
self because I bounced on her that night. I didn't care about her. I
used her. She got me dope, bought me clothes, a phone, an iPad.
She brought drugs to jail for me. I'm just starting to be able to un-
derstand, to feel that, and it's not comfortable. It's not good. But
I'm also happier than I've ever been in my life. I'm trying to figure
that out. I'm talking to my therapist about it, and my sponsor. I'm
working on it.

He tells me he feels guilty about Robin's death too, and it's all tangled up with his recovery and newfound joy, and I wonder if he
feels the vibrations of wonder—fear and beauty—stirring inside himself. I try to imagine what it must be like to feel an emotion you have anesthetized for so long it ceased to exist. If you kill
fear, you also kill beauty. We cannot perceive beauty unless we
also perceive its frailty. I don't tell him he's not culpable for their
deaths because he knows that intellectually, "but it's also part of
my wreckage," he says. "How I've treated people. I have to come
to terms with it." I wonder if he feels the need to justify why he's
still alive when Frances and Robin aren't. I am afraid to ask. Magical thinking takes many forms, and it's both useful and dangerous. He changes the subject, telling me about all the new muscles he's developing now that he works out regularly. I remember
clearly a day years ago during one of the worst periods of his drug
abuse. He was missing of course, somewhere on the streets in
Kensington, and I went for a hike to try and out-move my fear. It
was so simple as to sound cliché, but as I walked along the trail
in the dappled sunlight, noticing everything, feeling full of gratitude for the air, my long, working legs, the leaves floating to the
ground, I thought: "Why isn't this enough for him?"

[CLEAVE]

Now he tells me, "I never realized life could be so beautiful."

* * * * *

The waiting room is crowded with big windows that stretch to the ceiling. People drape or slump in their chairs in various states of distress. Those who have been here the longest are wearing sweatshirts and blankets. Some are bored, others laugh, a mother cajoles her kid again and again to eat something. A man in work boots and a hooded sweatshirt grips a National Geographic that he drops every time he falls asleep. Eric and I draw little pictures on napkins and guess what the other has drawn: a bulimic cow; a drunk potato farmer; Paris Hilton making a comeback as a talking purse.

It's too soon, only a couple of hours have passed, but the doctor is on the phone, the receptionist says, and he wants to speak to me. I feel my body rise but not the steps from the chair to the desk. Not the receiver in my hand. I don't register Mommom pressed beside me, or Aunt Carole's breath on my ear, or Eric's damp hand on my shoulder. I notice them later, in the still seconds after I hang up and turn to face my family.

"The surgery is done. It went well. She's in recovery and we can go see her soon." Mommom cries out and then covers her mouth with her hands. Her shoulders go slack, and Eric puts his arm around her. She slaps the receptionist's desk, which startles the receptionist, and says, "Let's go now." At eighty-six, she is pure, pulsing mother-love.

* * * * *

Every weekday morning, I make myself a smoothie with kale, kefir, cashews, and banana. I walk the one-eyed dog, then drive forty miles east down a flat highway into an egg-washed dawn peppered with crows. To the left are cornfields, to the right are flickering suburban tract homes. I try to picture myself living there—waking up and kissing my husband, listening to the kids fight in the bathroom—all that talking before breakfast. A few miles before the exit to Denison University are one of those new "lifestyle communities" catering to the "suddenly single" sect. Billboards project images of intimate, candlelit rooftop gatherings of attractive, diverse thirty-somethings laughing or sipping cocktails and donning hip headwear and nose rings. These condo developments are hugely popular around here, both in the city and in the suburbs, and often feature pools, gyms, rooftop bars, restaurants, retail space, yoga studios, eyebrow threading, and IV hydration therapy spas that will cure your hangover before your 9 a.m. meeting downtown. In Granville, the little Rockwellian village over which Denison looms like some munificent fortress, are tree-lined blocks adorned with nineteenth-century homes in Greek Revival, Federal, Tuscan, Victorian, or Colonial Revival styles. Each is pristine and garlanded with overflowing flower boxes and picket fences. The two blocks that compose the commercial district of town are Italianate, and feature the tavern, ice cream shop, coffee shop, candy store, popcorn shop, post office, and pharmacy. I can't imagine myself drinking a martini at my condo development's poolside bar any more than I can imagine pushing a stroller down Main Street and wearing culottes. My new life feels as undefined as the old one. And yet I'm in no rush. I know where I've been. I am the past and the future and ecstatically attuned to the present. I allow myself a brief memory of Jack when we were about twenty-three, newly graduated from college, and living together for the first time in New York City in a fourth-floor walkup studio apartment that we shared with a family of mice. It was early December and I was just getting home from my shift at the pirate-themed bar where I'd been working after quitting my job as a sixth-grade English teacher in Brooklyn. It was six in the morning and snowing. When I turned the corner onto our block, I saw Jack leaving our building, pulling the heavy red door closed behind him, dressed up for work in his new, shiny black loafers and wool coat. I was half-drunk and exhausted, and he smelled like must and Fructise shampoo. I stood on the step below him on the landing and lay my head on his stomach. He wrapped his arms around me, and we swayed there for a moment in the snow, onebody.

The sky here in Ohio is wide open and divested of mountains and sharp memories. Routine settles me—a daily, vinegary smoothie, walks with the one-eyed dog, my students filing in and out of the classroom, mumbling thank yous while dropping their essays onto the table. Essays about God and medical marijuana, justice and love, dead grandparents and grief, racism and violence, siblings and addiction, social media and insecurity, motherhood and sisterhood and brotherhood, romance and heartbreak. All the ordinary, extraordinary stories of the living. Sometimes they come to my office and cry. Sometimes we laugh. Sometimes we talk about holding conflicting truths in the same hand and knowing them to be equally true. Sometimes I go to the gym just to move my body in the company of other women's bodies. Once I went to the tailor just to be touched and I'm not ashamed. I'd do it again. Today I eat a turkey sandwich, look out of my office window at a bending oak tree, and marvel at my dumb luck. Just to be still enough to watch things grow. This is not the sputtering out of Aristotle's climax, only somewhere along the soft and endless circle of this one womanhood.

* * * * *

Too soon after that first cleaving, I turned seven. It was time for school. She put my hair in pigtails and my body in a sailor suit and we cried. There was school, sleepovers, sandwiches, and soccer practices. Boys to marry beneath the monkey bars and chase into closets. I read books about women and caves. About

girl bodies and boy bodies. The father came and went and died. I
grew plump, freckled, red-faced, and shy. Hair was everywhere
and never enough shelter. I learned to play the violin and smoke
cigarettes. I ate less and grew thin, met boys, did drugs, and
worshiped Virginia Woolf. There were biology classes, car rides,
black notebooks, waitressing jobs, aprons, pagers, piercings,
and a Korean boy named Lung who sucked my fingers under
the cover of his hooded sweatshirt during third period. There
were rivalries and petty gossip and too much makeup. Car accidents, hallucinogens, and karaoke bars in the city. Grown men
in the city. Teachers who would take you to the city for a night;
the bathroom for an hour. We buried the father, unpacked the
past. *Fuck you*, I explained patiently to anyone who would listen.
Then college, car payments, missed opportunities. Trips alone
to the Scottish Highlands and the corner store for six packs
at midnight. Met Rainbow People and celebrities, served cosmos, did cocaine. Became a nanny. Quit. Went home less often.
Then more. Then less. Wrote a book. Loved a man. Anticipated
death. Learned to fear phone calls and social media. Taught
classes. Went to the bar. Went to therapy. Went to the gym. Ad-
opted a dog. Went back. In the beginning, there was one woman
and she was light and dark and warm and humming and I did
not know where her body ended and mine began. She asks me
again one day, a year after my divorce, to freeze my eggs and I'll
agree to it, ever the good girl, still unsure whether it's for me or
her or the onebody we share. There's still time. Time to watch
the sun on my grandmother's upturned face as she smiles in
her beach chair. Time to run my hands through wet sand, my
brother's cries echoing in the distant past. Time to turn off the
light and run my hands over someone else's warm hips. Time to
kneel in front of frescoes in foreign cities. Time to sit beside Jessie in rocking chairs on the porch, laughing loudly into the endless night, the tethered dog licking our toes. Sometimes, I lay in
bed and imagine my eggs in the freezer, tiny universes secreted
in my body since before I was born, while I was still inside my

mother's body. And then her body, which had contained the egg that made me when she was still a fetus inside her own mother's body. And on and on and back and back. Generations of women carrying fragments of all the women who came before them and all the women who would come after, a strand of pearls.

[IN THE VALLEY]

JULY 2019

My father's story depends upon the image of his body bent over the bar inside the dark and narrow Valley Inn.

It's 1988, 1989, 1990, and by now he's been a regular at the Valley for a couple of decades, since he was a teenager, when he and my mother would hang there all night with their long-haired friends and all those good drugs. The Valley is tucked between a Chinese restaurant and a convenience store called Shiva, a single row of strip shopping in suburban Philadelphia. By now, the late eighties, friends have been replaced by kids, Eric and me, five and seven, and though we're not much for shooting the shit, we're at least self-occupied. Give us a couple of Shirley Temples and enough quarters for the pool table and we'll leave you to it. With chips of blue chalk, we draw war paint on our faces and fashion bows and arrows out of splintered cue sticks, rubber bands, and pencils fished from the bottoms of our bookbags. The expanse of green felt is our native land and we defend it fiercely, aiming our arrows at the big-bellied men in flannel who try to usurp the table, growling until they either walk away chuckling or give us money for the jukebox.

Those are the days of mustaches, mullets, Genesis nostalgia, and windbreakers. Of Bud Light, Marlboro Reds, and athletic socks. Of curtaining cigarette smoke swaying in the dim light of neon bar signs. And yet, what's interesting to me now about that image of the Valley is that my father is the most ephemeral part of it. I remember the red jars of pickled eggs better than I do my father's face.

Thirty years later, I'm back in the Valley. Nothing has changed. It is still, apparently, the days of mustaches, mullets, Genesis nostalgia, and windbreakers. The bartender smokes with one hand while with the other attempts a magic trick involving a shot glass, a stack of quarters, and a single match. The back room with the pool table is gone, closed off, but otherwise it may as well be 1989. Even the jars of pickled eggs remain, bone white and bobbing in a blood-red broth. The same big-bellied men in flannel hunch over the bar, the same feather-haired couples laugh gravelly over Bud Lights and two fingers of well whiskey. This isn't a story about irony. The quarters clatter to the bar and the bartender smiles shyly. She has two kids at home and a brand new Ford Focus to pay off. My father long ago drank himself to death; Eric is newly, precariously sober after fifteen years of heroin abuse; I've already had my first divorce and might have dried cum in my hair after a one-night stand; and my mother, here beside me, is down a lung after fifty years of smoking concluded in cancer and surgery a couple of months ago. We sip vodka tonics and pretend we're both not wishing we could bum cigarettes from the bartender, inside this smoky bar, while her remaining lung slowly expands to fill the new space in her chest. We're pretending, too, that we were just in the neighborhood, antsy after so many weeks stuck inside her house while she recovered, and not also trying to trace a history that started here, the two of them long-legged and pink-cheeked, laughing and doing lines in the bathroom, kissing between beers and pressing their little bellies together like moon pies.

The fact is that I've lived with memories of my father in the Valley far longer than I ever lived with my father. So, I wonder if my father *is* the Valley now. The Valley and my memories of the Valley. Maybe the memory of his body in the Valley grows more diffuse because the Valley itself is filling in the space where once there was a man, but now is just a story.

My mother is laughing, her face pale and shining behind a veil of smoke. "Just let me hold it," she says, reaching for the bartender's unlit cigarette and then dangling it limp between her pointer and index fingers. She presses it to her lips, pretends to inhale deeply, and smiles. Phil Collins sings *it's always the same, it's just a shame, that's all*, and somebody orders my mother another drink and they cheers to her health. The bathroom door slams shut, invisible children draw bows in the boarded-up back room, and the bartender balances quarters on a shot glass and strikes another match. My father glances at his watch and signals for another Bud. He wants to get home before his wife does, who will be tired after her double shift at the Hungry Pilgrim, but knows he probably won't make it. She hands the cigarette back to the bartender who puts it in her pack. I grab my mother's hand and squeeze. We watch the men float in and out of the Valley and try to breathe in the gusts of fresh air each time the door swings open. Later, she'll have to come pick him up in their old Honda hatchback, the kids will be half-asleep, their lips stained pink, and he'll walk back to the Valley alone after the kids are in bed, lean over the bar, and quietly evaporate.

In the morning, the nurse will arrive at eight to give my mother an enema, and I'll read pleading texts from the one-night stand while sipping coffee in the living room. My father will pull open the door to the Valley and step inside. He's wearing a jean jacket. Patting the top-left pocket, he checks on his wallet. His hair is soft and blond, not yet receding, and his eyes are blue and red-rimmed. His nose is crooked from the dirt-bike accident when he was fifteen, but the mustache distracts. "You know it's not a one-night stand if you keep in touch," my mother will say, unbuttoning her pants on the way to the bathroom, the young nurse close behind. He'll smile at the bartender who will sigh and pop open his beer, then pour whiskey in a shot glass while accidentally knocking over her stack of quarters. "Oh," my mother will call back, "your brother needs your Netflix password again." At closing time, my father will settle his tab in cash and tip with quarters and three Marlboro Reds. He misses his old truck, but he crashed it into a telephone pole decades ago. Breakfast, I'll decide, and head into the kitchen to crack eggs into a glass bowl. He'll stumble out into the shadows and by the time I've finished cooking, my mother will be back on the couch, breathing into a tube and trying to get the little blue ball to rise while the nurse cheers her on. My father leans against the Valley's brick facade, lights a cigarette, buttons his jacket, and then starts the familiar walk home.

[EPILOGUE]

On April 21, 2020, in the throes of the global pandemic, a girl-child came storming out of the ether. Charlie Helen Nelson. Eric's daughter. Though my mother and I could not be at the hospital for the birth, we witnessed her first days dizzily via FaceTime. As I watched my niece chirp and blink in my brother's arms, I felt a new kind of awe.

And that would be the end of this story, except true stories are never simple and never over. Eric relapsed a week later, then sobered and seemed to be doing well. He resumed his business and settled into a parenting routine with his partner and their daughter. I came back here, to Columbus. Then yesterday, June 25, 2020, he relapsed again. He sat on his bed in my mother's house and screamed while she tried to rid him of a half dozen pocketed needles and some bags of coke and pills. He ran outside and wailed into the sun. He threatened suicide. She called the cops. He swallowed a bottle of pills. He held a needle to his throat like a loaded gun. She rushed him to the ER.

Last we heard, he'd run from the hospital and is likely headed to Kensington. And all we can do is what we've always done: wait for the call.

*   *   *   *   *

I keep thinking about what my mother said almost a year ago
now, a hot afternoon in August, a few days after we'd learned
about the pregnancy. I was panicking, as usual, and expected my
mother to be doing the same. "How is he going to be a father?" I
said. "He can't even take care of himself. He has no money. He
only just got sober. He lives in a fucking halfway house, for god's
sake!" My mother was silent on the other end of the phone. I
paced in front of my apartment in Columbus, only half-aware of
the one-eyed dog eating his own shit in the garden. "Hello? What
are we going to *do*?"

She sighed. She was only three months out from her surgery and
her breathing was still labored. "Jess," she said. "We are not going to do anything. We have lived so long under the specter of
death. This is not perfect, but it is at least life."

And so she is, miraculous slip of girl, flesh and blood, Charlie
Helen.

And so I wait, here on my porch in Columbus, my apartment
in boxes, the ex-lover calling and calling, the job in Richmond
waiting. The wind kicks through the trees and I'm waving to
my neighbor who waves back and smiles behind her mask. She's
bouncing her newborn, who is swaddled to her chest, the sky
gone slate and electric in the summer heat. A pandemic surges.
An old truck idles at the corner. Behind us is the silenced city.
Ahead is everything else.